INDUSTRIAL POLLUTION

(A Reference to Small Scale Industries)

Authors:

N. SARADHA

M.A., M.Phil., M.Ed., Ph. D.

V. DHULASI BIRUNDHA

M.A., M.Phil., Ph.D., M.B.A., M.C.A.

SERIALS PUBLICATIONS

NEW DELHI

First Published - 2008

ISBN 978-81-8387-155-6

Published by

SERIALS PUBLICATIONS
4830/24, Prahlad Street, Ansari Road
Darya Ganj, New Delhi-110002 (India)
Phone : 23245225. Fax : 91-11-23272135
E-mail: serials@satyam.net.in

Contents

Acknowledgement

I owe a deep debt of gratitude to my Supervisor Prof. Dr. (Mrs.) V. Dhulasi Birundha, M.A., M.Phil., Ph.D., M.B.A., Dip. E.D., who guided me with her valuable advice, encouragement and inspiration. Her standard of accuracy, the illuminating corrections she made, the promptness with which she made them and the wise suggestions she offered, brought the work to its present shape.

I am deeply grateful to Prof. Dr. T. Valuthi Varagunasingh, M.Sc., M.Phil., Ph.D., Head and Co-ordinator, School of Economics, Madurai Kamaraj University, Madurai, for his advice and unstinting support during the various stages of this programme.

My sincere thanks are due to the authorities of Madurai Kamaraj University, Madurai, for the facilities provided, and for extending me the fellowship for pursuing the Ph.D. programme.

I wish to thank profoundly Dr. M.V. Nadkarni of ISEC, Bangalore, and Dr. Paul Appasamy of MIDS, Madras, for their valuable suggestions at the initial stages of the thesis work.

My sincere thanks to Prof. P.V. Ramachandran, formerly Head, Department of English, ICC & CE., Madurai Kamaraj University, Madurai, for helping me in the language aspect of this work.

I express my sincere and hearty thanks to the Directors of Small Industries Service Institute, Small Industries Development Corporation, Madras and the Manager of Economic Division, District Industrial Centre, Madurai, who readily responded with necessary information required for this research.

I also sincerely acknowledge the kind help extended to me by the members of the Advanced Environmental Laboratory, Tamil Nadu Pollution Control Board, Pasumalai, Madurai.

My thanks are due to Mr. P.V. Marimuthu, an Additional Manager, Environmental Laboratory, for his valuable information on technical matters.

I am grateful to all the library staff of ISEC, Bangalore, MIDS, Madras, CDS, Trivandrum, for their kind co-operation in making all required material accessible.

I express my sincere and hearty thanks to Miss. B. Angayarkanni and Miss. S. Manjula, who rendered timely help for the completion of this work.

I record my heartfelt gratitude to my parents and husband for their constant encouragement and help.

I also wish to thank Sri Balaji Computer Centre, Palkalainagar, Madurai, for the neat execution of computer printing of this thesis.

N. SARADHA

Foreword

The Ph.D., thesis entitled Industrial Pollution compiled by Dr. N. Saradha M.A., M.Phil., M.Ed., Ph.D., is an eyeopener for the Small-Scale industrialists in stressing the importance and value of social responsibility in maintaining the quality of the elements of environment in the industrial production. As our father of Nation, Mahatma Gandhi righly pointed out that *"we are the trustees of the earths' biosphere and not the owners"*.

The industrialists should pay equal attention in keeping the pollution to the minimum in the future. The products of pollution-free industrial process may fetch an attractive marketing in Global Market. The Indian Small Scale industrial products should move towards carrying the symbol *"Open Mouth Earthern Pot"*, on the label, the seal of pollution free process in coming years. This book directs towards that goal.

This book effectively covers the water and air pollution levels in the environment in and around the district of Madurai, in Tamil Nadu. The methodologies are well discussed and presented. This will be a pioneering work for future investigations. The subject of Environmental Economics is a new interdisciplinary area. The author has dealt with impact of cost of maintaining cleaner environment on the cost of production of commodities and services.

The author and her guide Dr. V. Dhulasi Birundha Ph.D., are to be congratulated for this valuable contribution. This valuable book should find a place in all Educational Institutions and Research Laboratories.

C. E. Sooriamoorthi

1

Introduction

It has been known from the Vedic times that nature and mankind form an inseparable part of the life support system. This system has five components - air, water, land, flora and fauna, which are interrelated and interdependent. They are co-evolved and co-adapted. Deterioration in one inevitably affects the other four. If the deterioration is for a short term, and the life support system has enough resilience, it repairs itself and reverts to the original state. But, if the period of deterioration is long, the whole system, including all life, is thrown out of gear.[1] The human exploitation of the natural resources at a greater rate than their regeneration, and the inputs not being put back into the natural eco-system, are responsible for environmental maladies.

There are different views regarding the origin of the pollution crisis on the planet earth. Many authors like Lynn White (1967) and Ian Mc Harg (1969) had blamed the Judeo-Christian ethic for pollution. According to them this ethic taught man to believe that the earth was made for him and he could do what he wanted with it. Such an attitude encouraged exploitation. This view was contradicted by Wright (1970) who postulated that it was not the religious belief but human greed and ignorance which had permitted human culture to develop an ecological crisis like the explosion of population.

Southwick (1976) has associated the human population explosion with the pollution problem. He postulated that with more people, there has been more sewage, more solid wastes, more fuel-burning and greater use of fertilizers and insecticides for increased food production. Some authors have blamed profit motive and capitalism of the capitalist countries like the U.S.A. and Britain for the rising pollution. But Russia, according to Izvestia, has been facing problems very similar to the Western countries like the severe oil pollution in the Caspian Sea from offshore oil drilling and flushing the holds of ships, and industrial pollution from milk, fish and linen factories, regional food combines and industrial complexes. It is clear that, in the case of pollution, the economic system is not the real culprit but the way man functions.

Modern ecologists like Odum (1971), Southwick (1976) and Smith (1977), regard factors such as human population explosion, unplanned urbanisation and deforestation, profit-oriented capitalism and technological advancement, as being responsible for the pollution crisis on earth. In fact, in countries having the greatest technological advances, the worst pollution occurs.[2]

Environmental problems are the leading issues of not only the highly-developed industrialised societies but of developing countries as well, pollution of air, water, land and marine sources, due to rapid industrialisation, is making human living hazardous day by day. Taking into consideration the unprecedented growth of population, urbanisation, ecological imbalance and deterioration, the concept of sustained economic development with due consideration of the environmental improvement is the need of the hour.

"A life of dignity and well-being becomes the inalienable right of all".[3] But planet earth today — stands self-condemned by environmental pollution, degradation and depletion. Industrialisation which is the barometer of civilisation is itself an instrument for environmental pollution which justifies the concept of 'growth with destruction'.

Any economic activity, industrial or agricultural, has a bearing on environment. As the pace of development picks up, production becomes a complex process and the use of non-reproducible resources and energy becomes more intensive. The impact might be economic prosperity; but the ravages on environment assume alarming dimensions.[4]

Life in the biosphere has been sustaining itself for more than a billion years. Though environment has tremendous capacities for recycling, there are also tolerance limits. When such limits are crossed a pollution crisis would set in.[5]

Man in pursuit of material gains forgets the fact that the earth does not belong to him; and that he belongs to the earth. And hence, he has a responsibility to safeguard all other species who share the same planet with him, and on whom ultimately his survival depends. On account of his nefarious activities, earth has been converted into an inferno of vastly poisonous gases threatening ultimately to doom human civilisation. Man of each generation should keep in mind that he has no right to impose an unreasonable burden on future generations of people who are not there to defend themselves.[6]

ECONOMIC DEVELOPMENT AND ENVIRONMENTAL QUALITY

Many developing countries in Asia had made all possible efforts towards industrialisation during the United Nations Development Decade of the 1960's. They considered that industrialisation was the panacea for all problems of economic development and that it would pave the way for a self-sufficient economy.

Actually industrialisation was recognised as the basis for development and all the developing countries were eager to modernise their industrial sector. Earlier industrialisation in developing nations was basically for extracting raw materials, many of them being non-renewable, for the markets of developed nations, where manufacturing took place. Later, the concept of industrialisation rapidly got transformed with the result numerous small scale and medium scale industries were set up. This growing momentum in industrialisation had decisive impact on environment.[7]

Industry is central to the economic growth in many modern economies. Many essential human needs are met through goods and services provided by industries, which extract raw materials from 'Nature' and discharge both 'Products' and 'Pollution' into the 'Environment'.[8] Greater the demand for goods and services from the industry, larger is the withdrawl of resources from Nature. Consequently, greater is the discharge of unwanted wastes into environment. If such discharges exceed the assimilative capacity of the environment, as evidently is the case at many places, pollution is only a natural and an inescapable consequence. Industries, therefore, whether big or small, low-tech or hi-tech, located in urban or rural areas, producing jugs or jets - all inevitably produce wastes and consequently are potential sources of environmental pollution.[9] Industrialisation leads to increase in pollution as effluents are discharged into rivers and noxious smoke and industrial flames into the air. The deterioration in the environment affecting the quality of life has assumed serious proportions. The question arises as to whether there existed a trade-off between the rate of economic growth and the rate of deterioration in environment.[10]

Industrial process invariably leads to the release of wastes which are not required by that industry. When such wastes are released outside the industry, they lead to the degradation of the environment. This is more so if these wastes are allowed to mix with river water.[11] The major types of industries that contribute significantly to pollution problems are tanneries, cotton-dyeing industries, paper and pulp industries, distillaries, dairies, fertilizers, electroplating, oil refineries and steel mills.

The impact of industry varies greatly from one sector to another and depends upon the structure of the economy in individual countries. It is significant that industries that consume more energy, water, wood, and other resources usually generate more residuals and pollutants. Some industrial activities affect not only the working conditions of their employees, but also the life of the entire communities. It has been proved experimentally that some highly toxic chemicals which are still in use today cause cancer, birth defects and long term genetic effects. Small Scale Industries tend to waste materials resulting in more pollution per unit of output than the large industries.[12]

SIGNIFICANCE OF SMALL SCALE INDUSTRIES IN NATIONAL ECONOMY

Besides setting up Large Scale Industries, the solution to unemployment and faster economic growth lies very much in the establishment of medium and Small Scale Industries for which capital requirement will be less but employment opportunities greater. Though there is ample scope for the expansion and establishment of traditional industries like textiles, sugar and cement, thrust should be on engineering, leather, electrical, rubber, dyes and chemicals, pharmaceuticals, minerals and automobiles. The vast sea-coast offers greater scope for a wide variety of chemical and other industries.

Small Scale Industries are recognized as instruments of social transformation, enlarged employment opportunities, broadcasting entrepreneurship and securing dispersal of industries. They have a strategic role to play in the economic development of industrially less developed countries like India.

The Bolton Committee observes: "One of the most important contributions of the small business to the community is in providing a wide range of choice and a high standard of personal service to the consumer".[13]

In India, the role of Small Scale Industries was adequately realised long back and it was reflected in the Industrial Policy Resolutions of 1948 and 1956. The Small Scale Sector has made a significant contribution to India's emergence as a world's tenth most industrialised nation. Both in terms of quantity and variety, small industries have come to occupy a prominent place in the national economy.

The development of Small Scale Industries helps in the diffusion of economic power and dispersal of wealth, so essential to achieve the egalitarian objectives of a socialistic society. It seeks to check imbalances between various states and between different regions of the same state. From only 16,000 units in 1950, the number of small scale enterprises had increased to 9.87 lakhs in 1987-88.[14]

The Small Scale Sector has a favourable capital-output ratio in comparison to the large sector. An investment of Rs.100 in fixed capital in an organised Small Scale Sector brings an output of Rs. 258 as against to Rs.110 in the Large Scale Sector, the value of output produced by the former being approximately 4.8 times that of the latter. Another feature associated with Small Scale Industries is that they are import-light that is, they use a relatively low proportion of imported equipment and material in relation to their total capital investment.

Nearly 75 lakh persons are directly employed by the small sector and they make up 38 per cent of the country's total industrial employment. It has a share of 40 per cent in the industrial output of units regulated by the Director-General of Technical Development. Small industries every year are claiming a larger share of exports.

The significance given to Small Scale Industries in the Indian context may be attributed to capital shortage and heavy pressure of population. Small Scale Industries adopt labour intensive techniques in which there is no necessity to have a high rate of capital formation which is suited to the Indian economy.

India has the second largest population in the world. It is facing acute unemployment problems. Small Scale Industries provide employment opportunities, thus minimising unemployment in India.

In 1982-83, a total number of 42,252 Small Scale Industrial Units were established. They increased to 1,57,892 units in 1992-93, which is more than three times, in Tamil Nadu. During 1993-94, 1,78,114 units of Small Scale Industries provided employment for 19.41 lakh persons.

District-wise and industry-wise registration of Small Scale Industrial (permanent) Units in Tamil Nadu as on 31.12.91 and district-wise details of registered Small Scale Industrial Units in Tamil Nadu as on 31.3.91 are given in Appendix - Tables A.1.1 and A.1.2.

POLLUTING INDUSTRIES

Many industries are producing waste effluents which cause pollution problems. The major types of industries that contribute significantly to pollution problems are tanneries, textiles, sugar, distilleries, dairies, fertilizers, pulp and paper industries, oil refineries, steel mills, pesticides, antibiotics, electroplating, chemical products, soap, rubber, plastic, paint and cotton-dyeing.

POLLUTION PROBLEMS OF SMALL SCALE INDUSTRIES

Pollution from Small Scale Industries individually may not create as much social impact as a bigger project, yet they do produce a wide-spread effect by virtue of their large numbers, inefficient operation, and inherent inability to respond to environmental imperatives. Pollution from Small Scale Industries therefore is not a matter for physical environment alone, but it has a much wider impact on socio-political and cultural fabric of the people.

Small Scale Industries do not require manufacturing licenses, and so they keep sprouting literally anywhere and everywhere. The consequent damage to the environment and to the society, could have been minimised or eliminated, had there been a mechanism of environmental safeguard, continues unabated. Far from proper location, Small Scale Industries even come up in congested residential areas, to the detriment of the neighbouring population.

The mad race for economic growth through industrialisation at the cost of environment would ultimately lead to disaster. If the present rate of pollution is not checked, then man will see, eat and breath pollution. So the solution lies in the harmonising of economic development with safe-guards for environment.[15] With the focus on prevention, innovation, low pollution technology, recycling and structural change, the concept of ecological modernisation gets based on the paradigm 'industry and environment' rather than 'industry or environment'.

SMALL SCALE INDUSTRIES IN MADURAI DISTRICT

Madurai District is one among the 24 districts in Tamil Nadu. In Madurai District, Small Scale Industrial Units had increased from 1,303 in 1981-82 to 5,579 in 1990-91 nearly four times in growth. In 1981-82, 9,778 workers were employed in small scale units. But the number of workers had increased to 36,647 in 1990-91. The output of Small Scale Industrial Units had increased from Rs.12,218.06 lakhs in 1981-82 to Rs.38,662.91 lakhs in 1991-92.

Taluk-wise details of permanent Small Scale Industrial Units with their investments and employment in Madurai District; trends in number of units in categories of Small Scale Industries and classification of registered Small Scale Industrial Units in Madurai District as on 31.3.96 are given in Appendix- Tables A.1.3, A.1.4 and A.1.5 respectively.

POLLUTION PROBLEM IN MADURAI DISTRICT

Environmental quality may get affected by developmental activities in urbanisation. These negative impacts on environmental quality in urban systems may be reflected in the form of deterioration in the air quality, water quality and solid waste dumping.

In Madurai, sources of water pollution are

(a) Industrial wastes,

(b) Human wastes and

(c) Sewage.

In Madurai almost 84 per cent of the borewell water is not fit for drinking as E.coli bacteria are present in the water. The Vaigai river bed and the banks have been encroached upon for various purposes. In the city region a larger number of open drains and other wastes enter the river. The river water is almost black in colour. Enchornia plants cover the water surface in the heart of the city showing entrophication. Organic wastes get added here.

In Vaigai river, the water pollution is very high. The main sources of pollution include open drainage, garbage dumping and run-off water from waste lands and fields and human excrement. Most of the ponds in Madurai are small, shallow and purely astalic. The pH of all the ponds is in the alkaline range, varying from 7.6 to 9.0.

In Madurai, air pollution is caused by automobile exhaust and firewood which is used as fuel in homes, hotels and industries. The NO_2 emission load from various sources are as follows: Automobiles form 65.3 per cent, domestic 24.4 per cent and industrial sources 10.3 per cent of the total NO_2 emission in Madurai city.

The unplanned growth leads to poor sewage facilities and stagnant waste water. Urbanisation produces positive impacts in terms of employment potential and diversity thus increasing chances for pollution. The industrial waste water flows from the factory into the ditches nearby. The foul smell of the waste water let during the evenings cause many health problems to the families living nearby.

NEED FOR THE PRESENT STUDY

The Small Scale Sector has the capacity to achieve certain socio-economic goals, particularly with regard to creating employment opportunities. It can function as a social strategy for integrating the agricultural and industrial sectors of the national economy. Small scale enterprises provide immediate large scale employment; they offer a method of ensuring a more equitable distribution of the national income and they facilitate an effective mobilisation of resources of capital and skill which might otherwise remain unutilised. Some of the problems that unplanned urbanisation tends to create will be avoided by the establishment of small centres of industrial production all over the country.[16]

P.C. Mahalanobis was of the opinion that "in view of the meagreness of capital resources there is no possibility in the short-run for creating much employment through the factory industries. Now consider the household or cottage industries. They require very little capital ... with any given investment, employment possibilities would be ten or fifteen, even twenty times greater in comparison with the corresponding factory industries".[17]

As far as Small Scale Industries are concerned, Madurai District occupies the sixth place in the whole of Tamil Nadu. There were 8,860 small scale registered units in Madurai District during 1992-93.[18] They provided employment for 57,716 people.

In Madurai District there are nine taluks. Among the nine taluks, Usilampatti is considered the most backward taluk. Andipatti, Uthamapalayam and Vadipatti Taluks are considered backward taluks. The remaining other taluks namely, Madurai South, Madurai North, Melur, Periyakulam and Thirumangalam are considered developed areas. The present study is concerned with the location and concentration of polluting Small Scale Industries in nine taluks. The study also tries to find the causes for concentration of small scale enterprises in the particular taluks.

Generally, the Small Scale Industries have adopted the labour intensive technologies. The recent trends of this sector's, capital productivity, labour productivity and capital-labour ratio are also to be studied. A comparative study of the growth of polluting Small Scale Industries located in Tamil Nadu State as a whole and Madurai District in particular has to be made.

Since environmental pollution by traditional and modern industries has been posing problems to the governments of developed and developing countries, the present study focuses on such problems. The Small Scale Industries selected by the Researcher for her present study are confined to the cotton-dyeing industry, electroplating industry and soap industry in Madurai District. The level of water pollution and air pollution created by these industries can be identified. However, an attempt has been made to study the problems in terms of their nuisance value to people residing near the factory units and in terms of their proneness to create occupational diseases of workers. The different aspects of the environmental problems of Small Scale Industries in Madurai District have not so far been thoroughly studied and analysed. Hence, the Researcher has taken up the study of problems of pollution generated by the Small Scale Industries in Madurai District.

Further, from the Researcher's point of view, a study of this topic would be immensely useful for the policy makers and environmentalists since industrial pollution is a universal problem, gaining much attention throughout the world. The Researcher has tried to suggest a few suitable remedial measures for proper environmental protection.

IMPORTANCE OF THE STUDY

At present, with growing number of industries, the consequent pollution of the environment and its resultant changes in the economic activities of the people have attracted the attention of the world. If pollution is not prevented or controlled at an early stage, its effects in terms of low quality products, poor standards of living and less hygenic conditions, will be harmful to the society. To control pollution caused by industries, it is necessasry to have information regarding the location of the industry, nature of the product, inputs used, the production process, cost of tne product, the existing technology for reducing pollution, and waste products and their effects on the surroundings. Hence, arises the need for the present study, namely an economic study of the industrial pollution caused by the Small Scale Industries in Madurai District.

There are a few reasons for selecting the Madurai District.

1. A large number of Small Scale Industries are functioning in Madurai District.
2. The polluting Small Scale Industries are concentrated in the Madurai District.
3. No attempt is made so far to study the pollution problem of the Small Scale Industries in Madurai District.
4. Some research has been conducted in the Madurai City but it is not applicable to the entire Madurai District and
5. Small Scale Industries particularly polluting industries have high growth rate in terms of number of units. There is an urgent need for studying their adverse impacts in terms of pollution.

Since the study analyses the various aspects of Small Scale Industries in terms of their water pollution, air pollution problems and their effects, it focuses on the very vital problem of the society, namely safeguarding the environment.

OBJECTIVES OF THE STUDY

The various objectives of the study are as follows:

1. To study the growth rate of polluting Small Scale Industries in Tamil Nadu in general and in Madurai District in particular.
2. To examine water pollution in selected industries.
3. To estimate the air pollution load in selected industries.
4. To assess the environmental impacts on workers and households and

5. To review the existing controls and regulation measures of pollution control implemented by the Government of Tamil Nadu Pollution Control Board in Small Scale Industries and suggest suitable policy measures to prevent pollution.

HYPOTHESES

Based on the objectives it is also proposed to test the following hypotheses that are framed.

1. Among the water polluting industries cotton-dyeing industry is a major polluting industry in Madurai District and
2. Air pollution in cotton-dyeing and soap industries is mainly due to firewood used as fuel.

LIMITATIONS OF THE STUDY

The Researcher has attempted to make a comparative analysis of the growth of polluting Small Scale Industries in terms of the number of units in Madurai District and Tamil Nadu. The data for Madurai District from 1981-82 to 1991-92 could be collected from the District Industrial Centre. But the data regarding Tamil Nadu were available for seven years only during the period 1981-82 to 1991-92.

Secondly, it was very difficult to study the relationship between location and concentration of industries and intensity of pollution, due to the lack of secondary data relating to the polluting Small Scale Industries separately from the aggregate data for the different categories.

Thirdly, the study was based upon the cross-section data of one year, 1991-92 and it is almost a static analysis. Excepting the few secondary data available from the offices, sufficient information could not be obtained from the factories on employment, income, pollution problem, pollution damage cost and pollution prevention measures employed. These factors also restricted the study to only a one-year period. Scientific attempts to measure pollution impact are even more recent and still incomplete.

Fourthly, the present study takes into account three categories of industry, namely cotton-dyeing, soap and electroplating. When the Researcher visited these factories it was found that they were generating both water pollution and air pollution problems. The chemical product industry and the paint industry were not studied in depth because they produce insignificant amount of pollution. They were taken into account only to assess their occupational hazards.

In the case of chemical product industry, pharmaceutical units in Madurai District are limited in number. Since they produce only tablets and syrups and not antibiotics they do not produce any type of pollution. The small scale paint units are just mixing the intermediate goods and produce the final product. Under these units there is absence of processing like stream washing, injection in which there is the possibility of waste effluents. At the same time paint industry may cause occupational diseases. The other units produce products namely flooring, colour oxide, sodium silicate, mixed fertilizer and the like which do not produce pollution problems. In the case of rubber and plastic industries, the raw materials are the old plastic materials which are converted into the new ones with the help of machines which crush them and reshape them. So there is no necessity of heating the plastic materials.

The respondents did not maintain any written account of their medical expenditure which is due to occupational diseases.

Fifthly, regarding secondary data, various agencies and government offices were not maintaining data in the way needed for this study. Hence, getting data proved difficult.

Sixthly, pollution being a sensitive topic, owners of polluting Small Scale Industries did not respond properly and come out with required information. They had to be persuaded by repeated visits.

SCHEME OF WORK

Following the introductory chapter stating the objectives and hypotheses, the second chapter deals with the Review of Literature, both theoretical as well as empirical.

The third chapter deals with Methodology used in this study.

The fourth chapter is devoted to the trend analysis of the growth of polluting Small Scale Industries in terms of number of units both in Tamil Nadu as well as in Madurai District within the eleven years taken up for study. It also deals with the location and concentration of polluting Small Scale Industries in Madurai District.

The fifth chapter is a profile of the sample units.

The sixth chapter describes the nature of water pollution created by the electroplating industry and the cotton-dyeing industry.

The seventh chapter discusses the nature of air pollution produced by the cotton-dyeing industry and the soap industry.

The eighth chapter identifies the environmental effects of pollution in Small Scale Industries on the workers and the households.

An examination of the existing controls and regulation measures of pollution control implemented by the Government of Tamil Nadu Pollution Control Board in Small Scale Industries and suggestions for suitable policy measures to prevent pollution are presented in the ninth chapter.

The tenth chapter is the concluding part of the work which furnishes the observations and recommendations.

NOTES

1. T.N. Khoshoo, "Environmental Concerns and Strategies", Ashish Publishing House, New Delhi, 1988, p. 3.
2. Timmy Katyal and M. Sataka, Environmental Pollution, (Ed.), Rajkumar, Anmol Publications, New Delhi, 1990, pp. 2-3.
3. J. Tinbergen, "Reshaping the International Order", A Report to the Club of Rome, 1976.

4. "Development and Environment", Founex Report, Development Digest, 10, 1972, p. 5.
5. Brown M. Douglas, Introduction to Urban Economics, Academic Press, New York, 1974, p. 271.
6. Rice Odell, Environmental Awakening : The New Revolution to Protect the Earth, Balinger Publishing & Co., Cambridge, 1980, p. 7.
7. Anandavalli Mahadevan, "Environmental Impact Assessment in Industrialisation", in Environmental Economics, Edited by Ghanshyam N. Singh, T. Valuthi Varagunasingh, N. Manonmoney and Kanti Singh, Mittal Publications, New Delhi, 1991, p. 261.
8. N. Manonmoney, "Environmental Problems in Developed Countries", Paper presented in the United Nations Environmental Programme held in Madurai Kamaraj University, Madurai, December, 18-22, 1989, p. 3.
9. K.P. Nyati, Problems of Pollution and Its Control in Small Scale Industries, Friedrich Ebert Foundation, New Delhi, June 1988, p. 2.
10. Edward Shapiro, Micro-Economic Analysis, Harcourt Brace Jovanvich Inc., New York, Fourth Edition, 1978, p. 389.
11. R. Krishnamurti, "Kaveri Basin Economic Development", Paper Presented in the Workshop conducted on behalf of The Department of Environment, Government of India, Science Foundation, Madras, p. 318.
12. K.P. Nyati, Op. Cit., p. 9.
13. S. Perumalsamy, Economic Development of Tamil Nadu, S. Chand & Company Limited, New Delhi, 1990, pp. 180-181.
14. J.C. Sandesara, "Modern Small Industry, 1972 and 1987-88- Aspects of Growth and Structural Change", Economic and Political Weekly, Vol. XXVIII, No. 6, February 6, 1993, p. 223.
15. G.S. Bajwa, "Problem of Environmental Pollution and Its Management in India", Edited by R.K. Sapru, Environment Management in India, Vol. II, Ashish Publishing House, New Delhi, 1987, p. 59.

16. Planning Commission, Second Five Year Plan, p. 47.
17. Quoted by Gunnar Myrdal in Asian Drama - An Inquiry Into the Poverty of Nations, Vol. II, Kalyani Publishers, New Delhi, 1985, p. 219.
18. Tamil Nadu - An Economic Appraisal, Evaluation and Applied Research Department, Madras, December, 1994.

2

Review of Literature

INTRODUCTION

A number of studies have been made on the economic aspects of environmental pollution and its effects on man and materials. This section attempts to review the earlier studies made on the location of industries, water pollution, air pollution and their economic effects. It consists of three parts. The first part deals with the various studies related to the location of industries. The second part presents the studies related to water pollution and its environmental impact and the third part deals with air pollution and its environmental impact. It specially deals with only two kinds of pollution - water pollution and air pollution. Other types of pollution problem like dust and noise are not severe in small industries. So many units among the Small Scale Industries do not have such problems.

STUDIES ON LOCATION OF INDUSTRIES

Sastry[1] who computed the 'Location Factors' with reference to industrial population and with reference to total population for the major industries such as cotton, jute, sugar, iron and steel, coal, cement and paper for the period between 1925 and 1937, observes that jute, iron and steel, paper, coal and cement are confined only to a few regions. Cotton industry is found in almost all regions and next comes sugar. He measured the changes in the locational pattern of Indian industries. It is further revealed that Bombay and Bengal stand out conspicuously in concentration of industries. But in some of the princely States like Baroda and Mysore, industries did expand rapidly so that their share of industrial workers was larger than the proportion of their population to the total population of the country.

According to Munshi,[2] the choice of location has been determined almost exclusively by business motives and that site has been selected which appeared to afford the greatest advantage to particular enterprise. The principal business motives and advantages were the growth of commerce at ports, entrepreneurial skills, nearness of raw materials, and the pattern of railway development. These led to the agglomeration at the principal ports which continue even to the present day.

In a report of Government of India,[3] it is stated that out of 35,783 small scale units registered in 1961, 22,457 or 62.85 per cent were located in the five developed States, namely Maharashtra, Gujarat, Tamil Nadu, West Bengal and Punjab. The share of these five States declined to about 52.26 per cent in 1966 and it further declined to about 44.63 per cent in 1972. The data relating to the number of registered small scale units show that the degree of concentration seems to have reduced over time.

Edward Benjamin's[4] study, "Economics of leather industry of Tamil Nadu with special emphasis on East India Leathers" reveals the fact that the location factor for 1970, for the tanning units in Tamil Nadu is mainly distributed among four districts. North Arcot is leading in concentration, with Chingleput coming next followed by Madurai and Trichy.

Following the methodology developed by P.S. Florence, location factors of nine industry groups for the five States

(Maharashtra, Gujarat, Tamil Nadu, West Bengal and Punjab) in India have been calculated by Godbole[5] for the year 1972. The nine broad industry groups selected from the total list of industry groups are the groups which contribute considerably to the total industrial activity and employment in the country. He computed the location factors for the nine industry groups for the five States - Gujarat, Maharashtra, Tamil Nadu, West Bengal and Punjab. He concluded that in Maharashtra, in seven of the nine industry groups the location factor is more than one while in Punjab it is so in five industry groups. In Tamil Nadu it is more than one in four industry groups while in West Bengal and Gujarat it is so in three industry groups. Maharashtra, Tamil Nadu and Punjab have thus substantial concentration of many different types of industrial activity.

Godbole[6] has also made an analysis of both absolute and relative concentration of industrial activity in the various regions. He has selected employment as the measure of concentration. He has used three different criteria to measure the size of industrial concentration in the States - factory employment, productive capital and value added. Increase ratings were calculated for the two periods, namely 1960-66 and 1966-70. The results indicate that in regard to magnitude rating between 1960 and 1970, there has been a reduction in industrial concentration in West Bengal on the basis of all the four criteria. In Maharashtra and Gujarat, there has been a reduction in respect of three criteria while in Tamil Nadu there has been reduction in regard to value added per employee. In Punjab the magnitude ratings have declined in respect of three criteria in 1970 as compared to 1966. Similarly, it is seen that there has been a decline in respect of some criteria in the increase rating during the period 1966-70 as compared to 1960-66 in all the developed States.

Renukarya[7] in his study on industrial dispersion observes that wide variations exist in the location of industries in Mysore District. Out of the eleven taluks, Mysore Taluk accounts for bulk of the industries. In fact 48.3 per cent of the industries are found concentrated only in this taluk. Yelandur has least number of industries accounting for only 1.83 per cent of the total industries in the district. The standard deviation is used as a measure of the spread of industries. The standard deviation is as high as 652.6 for the district which indicates very high regional imbalance in the location of industries. The study also points out the most important causes for heavy concentration of industries in and around Mysore and bleak dispersion in other areas.

STUDIES ON WATER POLLUTION

In their article entitled, "Effects of Certain Wastes on the Water Quality and Fisheries of Rivers Cauvery and Bhavani", Sreenivasan and Sounderraj[8] point out that the Seshasayee Pulp and Boards is a factory situated on the banks of the rivers near Erode. Effluents from all sections are combined and channelled for a distance of 3 to 4 kilometres. The effluent is dark brown in colour. The chief polluting agent of this region is its high Biochemical Oxygen Demand (BOD) varying from 100 mg/l to 1800 mg/l. There is a general increase also in the methyl orange and phenolphthalein alkalinity. The river Bhavani is subjected to pollution from the effluents of the South India Viscose Factory near Erode. The effluents of this industry are highly acidic. Free mineral acid as high as 280 mg/l is found. It has led to the destruction of molluses and virtual extinction of the bottom dwelling biota.

Sundaresan et al.,[9] in their study on water pollution revealed that in a well-operated and managed integrated pulp and paper mill the volume of waste water varies from 50,000 to 70,000 gallons for each tone of paper made. It was further revealed in their study that the biochemical oxygen demand discharged per ton of paper by kraft process varies from 34.5 to 64.5 kg. per ton of product. Straw board contributed 70 to 80 kg. per ton of product. Newsprint discharged 50 kg. BOD and current paper about 200 kg. BOD per ton. Small paper mills without soda recovery contribute about 236 to 400 kg.

BOD per ton of product. Besides, the strategy to control water pollution also had been suggested in this study.

Gaensler's[10] examination of a chronic lung disease occuring in textile workers engaged in carding and spinning room as a result of inhalation of cotton dust, revealed that in the U.S.A. 25 per cent of carders and 12 per cent of spinners had airway obstruction, indicating that upto 17,000 textile workers could have been affected. It is 63 per cent in U.K., 62 per cent in West Germany and 27 per cent in Egypt. In India several studies in the textile centres like Bombay, Ahmedabad, Kanpur and Madras were carried out by using the questionnaire method recommended by Schilling.[11] From these studies it was apparent that the incidence of lung disease in India was lower than in the west. It varied from 3.8 per cent to 8.4 per cent in various centres.

A study of treatment of paper and board mill wastes by Sastry and others[12] has shown how BOD and suspended solids could be significantly reduced from wastes by four alternative methods of treatment. It was revealed that the complete treatment cost varied from Rs.23.8 lakhs to Rs.42 lakhs.

In a report of Government of Karnataka[13] it is stated that industries are letting out their effluent into rivers or open grounds, which included Harihar Polifibres, West Coast Paper Mills, Mysore Paper Mills, Mandya National Paper Mills and The Binny Mills. Industries discharging effluent into the sea causing damage to acquatic life were the Caustic Soda factory, Karwar and Mangalore Chemicals and Fertilizers Ltd., Mangalore. As a result the river Thungabhadra has become polluted.

Atkins and Lowe[14] in their book "Pollution Control Costs in Industry - An Economic Study" state that textile dyeing unit creates water pollution in U.K. It dyes and bleaches lace and some nylon products. The unit used 4000 pounds worth of gas per month to heat the dyebaths and cleaning baths. The firm has a liquid effluent problem. It discharged 1/2 million gallons of water per week and this cost some 1500 pounds per year. Its effluent was not discharged direct into the sewers but went into a large drain in order that the acids and alkalis could neutralise each other. Even after the installation of this equipment (which costs 15000 pounds) the firm still had to pay 2000 pounds per annum as effluent charges based on the BOD, suspended solids and volumetric assessments.

As per the Report of National Environmental Engineering Research Institute (NEERI), 1971,[15] the river Damodar was found to contain 1,60,000 cubic meters of wastes discharged by eight major industries located on its banks. The effluents also contained toxic substances such as cyanides, phenols and ammonia. Pollution of Jamuna between Delhi and Agra has become a serious health hazard. The contamination comes from the wastes of the Dichlorodiphenyltrichloroethane (DDT) plants near Delhi. The Gomti River at Lucknow is similarly contaminated over a 35 km. stretch down stream from paper and pulp plant wastes and raw sewage. The Kalu river in Maharashtra is contaminated by nearly 100 industries, chiefly chemical and rayon, through sewers or streams.

Michael Roysten[16] mentions the pollution problem of two Japanese companies namely Mitsin Mining and Smelting Co. and Minamata Plant of Chisso Corporation, responsible for the Itai-itai disease. The disease acquired its name from the cries of the victims suffering from persistent pain due to the fracture of bones. The cause of the disease was found to be accumulated cadmium discharged from the former company, which polluted rice fields and well water. Organic mercury caused serious disorders of the central nervous system of persons who consumed large amounts of fish contaminated by effluents containing mercury discharged from the latter company. Since then a total of 115 deaths and 684 sick patients have been certified.

The scientific study of Shahul Hameed[17] points out that the wastes from tanneries, dyeing and chemical industries and distillery units are discharged into the Cauvery river affecting the quality of its water. He has analysed pH, colour, temperature, conductivity, total dissolved salts, chlorides and dissolved oxygen. Though this particular investigation points out that there is a high degree of pollution, it has not thrown any light on the influence of these effluents upon the biota of the ecosystem.

Backyavathy[18] in 1986 studied occupational health hazards of tannery and chromate industrial workers. She studied two groups - experimental group who were exposed to the occupational environment and the control group who were the family members of experimental subjects, not exposed to occupational environment. As far as the experimental group was concerned the occurrence of dermatitis was 8.6 per cent, bronchitis 32.8 per cent, acute pharyngitis 31.8 per cent, acid burns 3.6 per cent, asthma 2.8 per cent, allergic disorders 5.2 per cent, tuberculosis 2.6 per cent and injuries 36.2 per cent. Whereas in the control group the occurrence of dermatitis was 0.8 per cent, bronchitis 20.2 per cent, acute pharyngitis 5.8 per cent, acid burns 0 per cent (Nil), asthma 22 per cent, allergic disorders 2.6 per cent, tuberculosis 3.6 per cent and injuries 20.6 per cent.

As per the report of the Times of India[19] the river Cooum flowing in Madras has been polluted by sewage so much that not even the zooplanktons have been able to thrive in it. One litre of Cooum water has as much as 900 mg. of iron, 275 mg. of lead, 1313 mg. of nickel and 32 mg. of zinc. Besides heavy metals, very high levels of phosphates, silicates and nitrates also occur in the water. Sulphate levels ranging from 80-408 mg. were the highest recorded among Indian rivers.

Agarwal and Garg[20] mention about the observation of Piscator and investigation of Klein in their book. Piscator observed cases of chronic syndrome in workers in a Swedish factory due to the long-term exposure of cadmium oxide dust. The noxious influence of heavy metals on plants was described by Klein. It was found that all metals namely, Hg, Ag, Cu, Cd, Co, Cr, Ca, Fe, Ni, Pb and Zn were more concentrated in soils from industrial areas than in those from residential and agricultural areas. Due to the high concentration of these metals in these areas, vegetation got contaminated.

During 1977-79, the Central Ground Water Board[21] (CGWB) analysed the ground water in Ludhiana. It was found that the ground water in Ludhiana contained about 1-2 mg/l cyanide concentration due to the cyanide content in effluent discharges from the electroplating units. Similarly, where the tanneries were concentrated in some pockets in Tamil Nadu such as Chrompet, Ambur and Ranipet well water had been affected even at a distance of 1 km. from the tanneries with total dissolved solids rising to 1200 mg/l. In Rajasthan, the concentration of zinc, cobalt, silver and strontium in the ground water was found in excess of the permissible limit for drinking purpose. The effluent of Hindustan Zinc Ltd., in Debari and Khetri Copper Project were identified as the source for this pollution of ground water.

Sinha[22] in his article, "Effect of Waste Disposal on Water Quality of River Damodar in Bihar: Physico-Chemical Characteristics" states that wastes are discharged into the Damodar and its tributaries by as many as 29 industries in Bihar only. Calculating the industrial pollution load of the river it is estimated that the river is receiving daily 3,64,864 tonnes of suspended fine metallurgical grade of coal particles from wastes of 13 coal washeries and thermal plants. Besides, 16 tonnes of ammonia-nitrogen, 4.5 tonnes of urea-nitrogen, 0.8 tonnes of phosphate and 33.5 tonnes of sulphate are discharged into the River Damodar by the Fertilizer Corporation of India, Sindri.

Trivedy and Kulkarni[23] in their article on "Salient Features of Some Indian Rivers" observe that the water quality of river Ganga at Rishikesh is affected by 9,028 M3/day of antibiotic waste from Virbadra, antibiotic plant discharged into this river after treatment. At Kanpur, 45 tanneries, ten textile and several other industrial units directly discharge their untreated effluents in this river. The volumes of BOD load of these wastes are approximately 37.15 million gallons and 61,630.63 kg/

day in tanneries and textiles respectively. The BOD values have gone as high as 230 mg/l and bacterial counts are of the order of 400 to 2400 MPN/100 ml. Further the river Yamuna, the main source of water supply for Delhi, is heavily polluted. There are about thirteen big canals that discharge the waste in Yamuna. The Najafgarh canal contains high concentration of DDT and chloral hydrate affecting the river water and aquatic life. The load is of 15000 m^3/day of waste effluents containing 6000 kg/day of fixed dissolved solids, 300 kg/day of suspended solids, 3800 kg/day alkalies, 180 kg/day heavy metals, 300 kg/day of ink and dyes and 300 kg/day detergents. Several reports appeared from time to time in newspapers regarding heavy mortality of fish and the spread of epidemics of hepatitis due to heavy microbial pollution in the Yamuna river.

A preliminary study conducted by a team from the Central Board for the Prevention and Control of Water Pollution, New Delhi,[24] indicated that not all the industrial units in Chandigarh generated water pollution. 566 units out of the total 876 industrial units were classified as those generating some industrial effluents. Out of the 566 potential units which generated effluents, 262 units were in 'A' Category, that is, Mechanical / Engineering / Metallurgicals; 30 units in 'C' Category, that is, Electronics / Electricals and 274 units in 'D' Category, that is, chemicals. With a view to find out the total pollution generated from the industries, a pilot inventory survey was conducted by the Central Board team which covered 44 units. Those 44 units consumed about 3,150 KLD of water. The total number of 44 units were producing effluent volume 7720 KLD, BOD 1,073 kg/day and suspended solids 1,417.5 kg/day.

In their article entitled, "Some Aspects of Environmental Degradation of the Inland Open Water Capture Fisheries of Bangladesh", Syed Mohammed Iqbal Ali and Mir Waliuzzaman[25] point out that there is a large number of industries including tanning, glass factories, match factories, rubber factories, and glue factories along the bank of the river Buriganga in the Hazaribagh area of Dhaka District. All these industries dump their soiled waste and toxic effluent into the river. The maximum level of chromium and ammonia in the effluents of the tanneries recorded by Water Pollution Control Project in 1975 were 92.0 mg/l and 693 mg/l respectively. It reported high level of COD and BOD in the effluents of these tanneries.

Kalyanasundaram[26] states that more than 200 leather tanning units, located along the Palar river course from Ranipet to Vaniyambadi have flushed out such a volume of effluents over the years that the river is now called Pazhar (a river of waste), with the river water declared 'not potable' in many towns, and more than 20,000 hectares of land considered unfit for cultivation.

Malleswara Rao[27] observes that Hyderabad, surrounded by innumerable factories, has become a growing industrial monster. Toxic effluent was found in the douglas pouches of buffalo caracasses near the Patancheru industrial belt, where some 60 units are located, most of them chemical units discharging toxic wastes into three fresh water streams - the Nakkavagu, the Peddavagu and the Chinnavagu. The ground water in these villages has become so contaminated that lung, skin and other ailments have been reported. Cattle have perished, and birds, which used to flock in even from Siberia, have stopped coming and farmers have migrated. A saving grace is that all the pollution-causing units here had set up a three stage Rs.1.5 crore common effluent treatment plant which after completion of the second phase now has proved to be a success.

According to Roy Mathew[28] the pollution of the river Periyar is caused mainly by the discharge of effluents by industrial units and civic bodies. About 25 per cent of the units in the State are located along a 1 km. stretch on the Periyar bank at Udhyogamandal. They discharge poisonous pollutants containing heavy metals such as zinc, mercury and copper and flourides and phosphates. The discharge by 11 major units alone comes to 1.3 lakh kilo litres. Though the State Pollution Control Board has a unit to monitor the pollution, it is not effective. It is said that some factories let out their toxic effluents during night when the monitoring station is not working.

Ramakrishnan[29] observes that the death of nine buffaloes in a canal in Kodungaiyur in North Madras was due to cyanide poisoning. A large cycle manufacturing company had dumped the cyanide waste from its electroplating unit in the canal. Many corporation workers fell ill after they got into the canal to clean it. There are over a 100 electroplating units in the city, dumping their cyanide waste without any regard for public safety. The wastes are either let into the sewerage system or in convenient places.

STUDIES ON AIR POLLUTION

Sundaresan et al.,[30] have explained the magnitude of air pollution and monitoring air quality. They argue that sulphurdioxide, oxides of nitrogen and suspended particulates have been identified to be some of the major pollutants in industrial regions as well as cities. Besides, emissions from some of the industries have become a source of nuisance and have damaging effects on neighbouring factories and emission control at the source in each factory has now become inevitable.

In the Annual Report of the Administrator of the Environmental Protection Agency[31] it is revealed that the petroleum refining industries is the largest single source of emissions. In 1967 they accounted for some 11.9 million tons of emissions. Other industries with large amount of emissions include gray iron foundaries and units manufacturing copper, iron and steel articles. At the other extreme, secondary non-ferrous metallurgy industries and units manufacturing aluminium articles and nitric acid had relatively low emission levels in 1967.

Dewees and Others[32] have mentioned about the incidence of lead pollution. It has been alleged that the Toronto Refiners and Smelters Ltd., is a source of 'excessive lead contamination' upto a distance of five hundred feet from the property line and that the occupants of these houses live in an environment of above normal lead concentration. The evidence suggests that high suspended lead levels (710 mg/gram) exist only in areas very close to the plant. This can be explained largely by fugitive dust emissions from battery crushing operations and materials handling. Since the particulates emitted from these operations are rather large they stay airborne only for short periods.

Kothari[33] has quoted the report of the Ministry of Labour in his address in the National Seminar. Concentration of silica dust greater than 5 P.P.M. per c.ft. of air is highly injurious. In India, several surveys have been carried out by the Ministry of Labour to determine the incidence of silicosis. In potteries and ceramic industry, it was found that 15.7 per cent had X-ray evidence of silicosis. In coal mines in Bihar, 18.8 per cent incidence has been reported. In mica mines, 34.1 per cent incidence has been reported.

In his article entitled, "Environmental Problems - A Bird's Eye View", Ravi Sharma[34] observes that India's main problem of air pollution is due to the fact that 80 per cent of her industrial production is concentrated in 8 or 10 large industrial centres forming isolated pockets. Calcutta is found to be the most polluted city in India where carbon monoxide concentration is the highest in India. The Gorakhpur and Ahmedabad fertilizer factories cause air pollution due to fuel gases, like, CO_2, CO, SO_2 and dust. Leakage of ammonia further adds to pollution from urea plants. The Neyveli Lignite Complex in Tamil Nadu causes air pollution by dust, smoke, grit, SO_2 and CO.

Air pollution causes coughing, sneezing, thickening and secretion of mucus and narrowing or complete closure of glottis due to the presence of gases. This is true especially in the case of SO_2, Nitrogen dioxide and the oxidants. The frequency of fogs, incidence of respıratory diseases, suffocation and discomfort can be felt as a result of the heavily polluted atmosphere. It is significant that one study showed that a chronic exposure to SO_2 and NO_2 had an effect on the mortality rate from cancer. Polycyclic Aromatic Hydrocarbons (PAHs) are found to be related to the pathogenes of lung cancer. Chronic bronchitis and emphysema have also been found to be caused by excessive exposure to SO_2. Carbon monoxide in congested areas removes 5 to 10 per cent of the blood from circulation.

While observing the medical cost of a polluted environment, Michael Roysten[35] indicated that a study done in the United Kingdom put the national health cost of air pollution in 1970 at 640 million pounds, the majority of these costs being attributable to bronchitis. Various studies concerned with respiratory diseases in other countries have indicated that 20-50 per cent of all cases of bronchitis could be attributed to air pollution, as also 20-25 per cent of all cases of lung cancer. On the basis of such estimates, a Canadian study has shown that a total of 6,60,000 mandays a year are lost through pollution - induced bronchitis. In the United Kingdom in 1970, the total was nearer 10 million mandays, leading to an estimate of 45 million being the value of productivity lost for this reason. In the U.S.A. it has been estimated that half of the deaths from bronchitis can be attributed to air pollution.

K. Adinarayana Reddy in his article on "Environmental Issues and Planning Considerations: A Case of Calcutta" has given the report of Calcutta Metropolitan Development Authority (CMDA).[36] According to CMDA estimate at present (1984) there are more than 6000 units of medium and Large Scale Industries, around 52000 Small Scale Industries, over 27000 furnaces and 5000 tanneries in Calcutta. These industries alone emit 1084 tonnes of polluted matter. They emit toxic gases and pose a great danger to human health and hygiene. The statistics further show that about 25 per cent of the deaths in the city could be attributed to respiratory diseases.

Patel and Pondey[37] have analysed air pollution in their book, "Determination of selected metals in Flyash fallout from Thermal Power Plant". They point out that the fallout rates of settleable particulate plant of flyash matter emitted from a thermal power plant of 540 MW capacity have been measured by setting up 20 sampling stations in an area of 64 km. in the vicinity of the power plant. The dust fallout was found to be in the range from 264.84 to 848.18 t/per sq.km. per month. Results are used to assess the magnitude and rates of entry of these metals into the soil horizon in the vicinity of the plant.

According to Sushil Kumar,[38] a Swiss-owned chemical plant at Seveso, Italy exploded and a cloud of toxic dioxin was released into the atmosphere. An area of about 20 km. radius around the plant was damaged and the loss was estimated at around 28 million dollars. The entire livestock and crops in the contaminated areas were destroyed during clean-up operations. Nearly 500 people died and thousands were injured due to a gas explosion and fire at a storage plant in Mexico. Pemex, Mexico's State Oil Company, was officially blamed for the disaster.

Swaminathan and Sundaresan[39] presented a paper relating to Auto Exhaust emissions in India in the year 1980, at WHO/UNEP Biregional Workshop on "Planning for Control of Emissions from Motor Vehicles", at Kualalumpur. They state that of the total emissions in India (23,412 million tonnes per annum) the industries, domestic sector and automobiles contribute 63.42 per cent, 29.82 per cent and 6.76 per cent respectively.

In their article entitled, "The Air Act, 1981 Lacunas and Remedies", M.R. Garg and N.S. Tiwana[40] remark that sulphuroxide can cause temporary and permanent injury to the respiratory system, irritating the upper respiratory tract and lung tissues. Photochemical oxidants result in eye irritations and studies indicate that nitrogen oxides are harmful to human health, specially increasing children's susceptibility to 'flu. Air pollution has inflicted wide-spread damage on plant life, buildings and materials. Air pollutants also damage man's durable products; steel gets corroded 2-4 times faster in urban industrial centres than in rural areas. Sulphur oxides also accelerate the erosion of buildings throughout the world, as ozone accelerates the cracking of rubber.

Abubacker[41] studied in 1990, the socio-economic impact of pollution created by cement factories. He estimated the cost of environmental damage by assessing the degree of pollution, which is measured as the deviation of actually measured level of cement particulate in the vicinity of the household. Larger the deviation, higher would be the degree of pollution and lesser would be the environmental quality. Results of data analysis show that the cement pollution exceeded the tolerance limits and affected the health of human beings and agricultural yields of the study area. Cost analysis results have proved that prevention of pollution was more advantageous socio-economically than allowing damage to be caused and then remedying it.

Lal and Ambasht[42] have made a study of effects of cement dust on guava plants near Churk cement factory. The plant leaves received cement dust at the average rate of 1.24 g/m^2 per day. The maximum cumulative load reached upto 47.5 g/m^2 in January. In dusted leaves the chlorophyll content was higher but the leaf biomass was lower than in the plant leaves which were free from cement dust.

Mariappan[43] in 1990 studied air pollution, water pollution, noise pollution and solid waste pollution in Madurai City. He says that the industrial development and increase in number of industries in and around Madurai City are the major causes for air pollution. In 1976-77, the number of industries was nearly 1800, but it has increased to 6556 in 1989-90. SO_2 present in the atmosphere around the Kochadai area and the western side of the city was due to the operation of two major rubber industries. According to his findings, the cause for water pollution is mainly the improper behaviour of industrialists and also the careless behaviour of the people. For noise pollution, the transport sector and for solid waste pollution, the improper municipal waste collection method are the major causes. This study reveals that the health of the city people has been highly affected more by water pollution than by any other like solid waste, noise and air pollutions.

He has suggested that the environmental problems particularly those caused by harmful effluents might be redressed through regulatory mechanisms such as permits, establishing minimum standards of water or air quality or specifying the treatment equipment to be used.

Ramasubramanian's[44] study on "Health Condition of India Cement Factory Workers in Sankarnagar" reveals the fact that tuberculosis prevalence was maximum among the kiln workers (46.66 per cent) and its occurrence was found to be in persons of age 30 and above. Coughing symptom frequency was found to be high among packing house workers (27.27 per cent) and its presence was common among all the age groups irrespective of service. Breathing trouble and upper respiratory tract infection was found to be maximum among packing house workers (30.3 and 28.57 per cent respectively) and breathing trouble was found among the workers in the age group of 31 to 40 and above. Upper respiratory tract infection was widespread among all the age groups.

While making observations on Environmental Disaster, Baruch Fischhoff[45] states that Krakow was once the capital of Poland and it was adversely affected by air pollution. The buildings and statues were eaten away by acid rain. The most identifiable source of air pollution in Krakow was the Nowa Huta Steel Works. 80 per cent of the workers retired because of disability. Human life expectancy was falling while the rate of leukemia was rising around Krakow. Infant mortality was increasing. The people had constant respiratory problems. It was uncommon to find someone with a red blood cell count above the norm of 5 million per cubic millimeter, despite high levels of carbon monoxide in the air, which typically increased red blood cell counts.

Neena Vyas[46] observes that there are also about 60000 to 70000 Small Scale Industrial Units in Delhi, often in ill-ventilated sheds. Even the bigger units do not have equipment to treat their dangerous effluents and wastes. It is estimated that 1172 tonnes of suspended particles, hydrocarbons, sulphur dioxide, nitrogen oxides, carbon monoxides and other poisonous gases are spewed into the air in Delhi by industrial units, various modes of transport and power stations.

While observing the big problems of Chotanagpur Ramesh Upadhyaya[47] states that major and medium irrigation-cum-hydel projects would aggrevate the problem of environmental pollution and result in large scale displacement of the tribals. An enormous quantity of ash from the Chandrapura Thermal Power Station of the Damodar Valley Corporation - an estimated 80,000 tonnes of ash flows into the Damodar.

Ramdas[48] in his article on "The Fly Ash Menace" states that more than 2500 tonnes of fly ash is generated daily and this is expected to go up several times after the superthermal plants and a fertilizer plant of the National Thermal Power Corporation are commissioned and the National Aluminium Company adds its sixth unit. Though the installation of efficient Electro Static Precipitators (ESPs) would reduce the fly ash emission by some 95 per cent, the remaining is enough to cause concern. NALCO has not only provided ESPs, but has acquired over 320 hectares for an ash pond. In smelters, the common and most hazardous pollutant is fluoride used as sink. The flouride emission problem becomes acute especially where smelters are located near agricultural land. The reported increase of flouride content in drinking water around NALCO's smelter plant is also causing a lot of concern. Also, prolonged exposure to high level of flouride emissions causes flouriosis and loss of appetite especially among children.

Dhulasi Birundha Varadarajan and Anandhavalli Mahadevan[49] have analysed the economic and environmental impact of fuel consumption pattern in Small Scale Industries in Madurai Corporation zone. Though a larger percentage of industries use electricity as the major fuel source, in terms of absolute energy value, it forms only 7.5 per cent of the total energy consumed. While firewood contributes as high as 67.7 per cent of energy, furnace oil shares only 12.6 per cent, kerosene and diesel supply less than 1 per cent of energy. Based on the diversity and quantum of fuel utilisation, the general environmental impact caused is assessed. The fuels consumed by the industrial units are capable of generating air pollution. It is further revealed in their studies that firewood produces a very high quantity of particulates and sulphur-dioxide. Next to firewood coal produces larger quantities of pollutants. This will have an adverse effect on the community, air quality and hence on public health.

Baskaran's[50] study on "Environmental Impact of Cement Industry with reference to Madras Cements Limited" reveals the fact that the residents have only low and medium impact levels. It is found that the occupation of the residents influence the impact level whereas the age factor does not. He has attempted to study the impact of cement dust on farming operations. It is further revealed in his studies that most of the farmers have medium impact level followed by low impact level and a few only have high impact level. The study confirmed the impact of cement on farming operations with respect to the following components:

1. Reduction in agricultural income,
2. Fall in crop yield,
3. Reduction in quality of the yield and
4. Increase in the cost of cultivation.

He has suggested the ways and measures to solve some problems in cement industry relating to air pollution.

In his article entitled "Potentially Explosive - Visakhapatnam", Sampath[51] refers to a survey conducted by the National Environmental Engineering Research Institute (NEERI). According to the Survey, the pollution levels were quite high. The dust fall recorded at the Town Hall varied from 114 to 174 tonnes per sq. km. per mensem as against the permissible level of only 10 tonnes per sq.km. a month. The suspended particulate matter was found to be 204 to 213 micro grams per cubic metre a day in the industrial estate. As for the sulphurdioxide levels recorded, it was 127 micro grams at Town Hall and 139 micro grams in the Port area. The pollution was caused by the major units: Hindustan Zinc Limited, Coromandal Fertilizers Limited, Hindustan Petroleum Corporation Limited, Visakh Refinery, Coastal Chemicals Limited, Godavari Fertilizer and Chemicals Limited and Hindustan Polymers of the United Breweries Group. As such most of the people in the city and those particularly in the neighbourhood of industrial units were exposed to air pollution that caused headache, dizziness, cough, cold, sore throat, eye irritation, dermatitis, bronchitis, asthma, allergies, muscular pains, spasms and respiratory and cardio-vascular ailments.

Mehta[52] observes that the greatest polluter causing damage to the Taj Mahal has been the refinery at Mathura. This refinery is permitted to emit from its Chimneys 24000 kilograms of sulphurdioxide per day. It is totally arbitrary and no attempt has been made thereafter to review the situation.

Thus, the review of the earlier studies reveal the fact that severe environmental damage like air pollution and water pollution are caused due to the concentration of industries in a particular area. The health hazards are also the result of these industries. Though the magnitude of the problem differs from one area to another, the general underlying observation of these studies is that the rapid industrial growth unmindful of its impact on environment is a threat to humanity. More and more micro level studies are warranted for specific policy guidelines.

NOTES

1. N.S.R. Sastry, A Statistical Study of India's Industrial Development, Thacker & Co., Bombay, 1943, pp. 40-42.
2. M.C. Munshi, Location of Industry: Evolution of a Policy in Industrial Development in India, Edited by C.N. Vakil, Orient Longman, 1973, pp. 40-42.
3. Small Scale Industries Hand Book of Statistics, Small Scale Industries, Government of India, New Delhi, 1973, p. 40.
4. R. Edward Benjamin, "Economics of Leather Industry of Tamil Nadu with Special Emphasis on East India Leathers", Unpublished Ph.D. Thesis, School of Economics, Madurai Kamaraj University, February 1979.
5. M.D. Godbole, Industrial Dispersal Policies, Himalaya Publishing House, Bombay, 1979, pp. 5-9.
6. Ibid., pp. 5-9.
7. C.K. Renukarya, "Industrial Dispersion: A Case Study of Regional Disparity", Edited by B.S. Sreekantaradhya, Regional Dispersal of Industries and Industrial Development, Deep and Deep Publications, New Delhi, 1985, pp. 155-162.
8. A. Sreenivasan and R. Sounderraj, "Effects of Certain Wastes on the Water Quality and Fisheries of Rivers Cauvery and Bhavani", Environmental Health, Vol. 9, 1967, pp. 13-27.
9. B.B. Sundaresan, R. Pitchai and C.A. Sastry, "Air Pollution in Madras City", Edited by K.M.S. Benjamin, Dimension of Environment with Special Reference to Condition in India, Centre for Human Development and Social Change, 1971, p. 15.
10. E.A. Gaensler, "Environmental Lung Disease", Medical Clinics of North America, Vol. 57, 1973, pp. 593-595.
11. R.S. Schilling, "Byssinosis in Textile Industry", Journal of Environmental Health, Vol. 21, 1970, pp. 475-478.
12. C.A.Sastry, S.R. Alagarswamy and V.Kothandaraman, "Treatment of Paper and Paper Board Mill Wastes - A Case Study", Indian Journal of Environmental Health, Vol. 16, No. 4, October 1974, pp. 317-335.

13. Karnataka Legislative Assembly, Report of the Committee on Government Assurances to Legislative Assembly on Industrial Pollution, Bangalore, 1976.
14. M.H. Atkins and J.F. Lowe, Pollution Control Costs in Industry - An Economic Study, Pergamon Press, Oxford, 1977, p. 137.
15. As reported in Desh Banthu and Eklavya Chauhan, Current Trends in Indian Environment, Today and Tomorrow's Printers and Publishers, New Delhi, 1977, pp. 31-32.
16. Michael Roysten, Pollution Prevention Pays, Pergamon Press, Oxford, 1979, pp. 34-35.
17. M. Shahul Hameed, "A Report on the Hydrobio-logical Conditions of the River Cauvery and the Industrial Effluents in and around Tamil Nadu", Memoirs of the Salem Institute of Experimental Biology No. 1, 1981, pp. 246-251.
18. D.M. Backyavathy, "Epidemiological, Environmental and Toxicological Studies on Tannery and Chromate Industrial Workers of Ranipet Industrial Town and Its Environs", Unpublished Ph.D., Thesis, S.V. University, Tirupati, 1986.
19. The Times of India, May 27, 1987.
20. S.K. Agarwal and R.K. Garg, Environmental Issues and Researches in India, Himanshu Publications, Udaipur, 1988, p. 168.
21. As reported in T.N. Khoshoo, Environmental Concerns and Strategies, Ashish Publishing House, New Delhi, 1988, p. 91.
22. As mentioned in R.K. Trivedy, Ecology and Pollution of Indian Rivers, Ashish Publishing House, New Delhi, 1988, pp. 220-231.
23. Ibid., pp. 396-400.
24. Central Board for Prevention and Control of Water Pollution, Preliminary Report, 1981-82 on U.T. Chandigarh, p. 29, as presented by I. Mohan, Environmental Pollution and Management, Ashish Publishing Company, New Delhi, 1989, pp. 310-312.
25. As found in M.M. Jana, Environmental Degradation and Developmental Strategies in India, Ashish Publishing House, New Delhi, 1991, p. 111.
26. N. Kalyanasundaram, "Facing Threat on Several Fronts", The Hindu, Survey of the Environment, 1991, p. 72.

27. M. Malleswara Rao, "Andhra Pradesh - A Growing Industrial Monster", The Hindu, Survey of the Environment, 1991, p. 66.
28. Roy Mathew, "Kerala - A Controversial Project", The Hindu, Survey of the Environment, 1991, pp. 69-71.
29. N. Ramakrishnan, "Madras : Troubled Giant of South", The Hindu, Survey of the Environment, 1992, p. 75.
30. B.B. Sundaresan, R. Pitchai and C.A. Sastry, Op. Cit., p.4.
31. Donald T. Savage, Melril Burke, John. D. Coupe, Thomas D. Duchesneau, David F. Wihry and James A. Wilson, Economics of Environmental Improvement, Houghton Mifflin Company, Boston, 1974, pp. 36-37.
32. D.N. Dewees, C.K. Everson and W.A. Sins, Economic Analysis of Environmental Policies, Toronto Press, Toronto, Canada, 1975, p. 142.
33. J.C. Kothari's Paper entitled, "Lung Disease in Industry" in the Proceedings of the National Seminar on "Industry, Environment and Man", 8-9 February, 1975, Organised by The Central Labour Institute and the Society for Clean Environment, Bombay, p. 143.
34. Ravi Sharma's article in Desh Bandhu and Eklavya Chauhan, Current Trends in Indian Environment, Today and Tomorrow's Publishers, New Delhi, 1977, p. 28. p. 170.
35. Michael Roysten, Pollution Prevention Pays, Pergamon Press, Oxford, 1979, pp. 27-28. p. 168.
36. CMDA, "C.M.D. Information", Calcutta, 1984, p. 24.
37. "Parayavaran Abstracts", Department of Environment and Forests and Wild Life, Environmental Information System, Vol. II, New Delhi, 1985, pp. 9-11.
38. A. Sushil Kumar, "Towards Strict Liability", Economic Times, 2 February 1986, p. 4.
39. As mentioned in Uma Melkania and N.P. Melkania, "India's Environmental Concern", Published in Environmental Pollution and Management, Edited by I. Mohan, Ashish Publishing House, New Delhi, 1989, p. 8.
40. As quoted by I. Mohan (Ed.), Environmental Pollution and Management, Ashish Publishing House, New Delhi, 1989, pp. 190-191.

41. M.H. Abubacker, "Socio-Economic Impact of Pollution: A Study of Cement Factories in Tiruchirapalli District, Tamil Nadu", Unpublished Ph.D. Thesis, Bharathidasan University, Tiruchirapalli, 1990.
42. R.S. Ambasht, Environment and Pollution, Students, Friends & Co., Lanka, Varanasi, 1990, pp.155-156.
43. M. Mariappan, "A Study of Environmental Pollution in Madurai City", M.Phil. Unpublished Thesis, School of Economics, Madurai Kamaraj University, Madurai, April, 1990.
44. A. Ramasubramanian, "Health Conditions of Workers - An Assessment Based on Dust Pollution in India Cements Limited, Sankarnagar, Nellai Kattabomman District", Unpublished M.Phil. Dissertation, School of Economics, Madurai Kamaraj University, Madurai, April, 1990.
45. Baruch Fischhoff, "Science and Politics in the Midst of Environmental Disaster", Environment, Heldref Publications, Washington, Vol. 33, No. 2, March 1991, pp. 13-14.
46. Neena Vyas, "In the Pollution Capital", The Hindu, Survey of the Environment, 1991, p. 53.
47. Ramesh Upadhyaya, "Big Problems of Chotanagpur", The Hindu, Survey of the Environment, 1991, p.51.
48. N. Ramdas, "The Fly Ash Menace", The Hindu, Survey of the Environment, 1991, p. 66.
49. Dhulasi Birundha Varadarajan and Anandavalli Mahadevan, "Economic and Environmental Impact of Fuel Consumption Pattern in Small Scale Industries", Edited by V.S. Mahajan, Studies in Energy and Economic Development, Deep & Deep Publications, New Delhi, 1991, pp. 257-265. p. 168.
50. M. Baskaran, "Environmental Impact of Cement Industry with reference to Madras Cements Limited", Unpublished M.Phil. Dissertation, School of Economics, Madurai Kamaraj University, Madurai, 1992.
51. R. Sampath, "Potentially Explosive - Visakhapatnam", The Hindu, Survey of the Environment, 1992, pp. 109-111.
52. M.C. Mehta, "Taj Trapezium: A Wonder Under Smog", The Hindu, Survey of the Environment, 1994, p. 59.

3

Methodology

INTRODUCTION

This chapter discusses selection of study area, the sampling procedure, collection of data, various methods adopted for analysis and concepts used. It describes the methodology followed in this study.

DATA COLLECTION

To analyse the objectives, two kinds of data were required. To examine the water pollution load and air pollution load, primary data pertaining to production particulars, fixed capital, labour employment, profit and loss, input materials used, consumption of energy, quantity of residues generated per day, raw materials used per day, quantity of effluent let out per day, disposal and treatment of effluents, solidwaste disposals, extent of air pollution load, facility available for testing waste water, cost of pollution control devices and related expenditure for existing schemes and awareness of pollution control policy from each factory were collected from the authorities of the Small Scale Industries. These data were obtained through direct personal interviews.

In order to assess the environmental impact on polluting small scale industrial workers, details of working experience, diseases affecting workers along with their names, duration, treatment and cost, extent of cure, medical leave applied, medical aids availed from the factory and other agencies, provision of protective materials and facilities inside the factory were required. General principles were adopted in framing the questionnaire. Before the final form of the questionnaire was adopted, a pilot survey was conducted in order to identify the drawbacks of the questionnaire. The work of pre-testing the questionnaire was done with utmost care and caution. The data were collected through the direct personal interview method. The information obtained was first-hand and original in character.

To study the environmental impact on households near polluting units, details of diseases, their nature and duration, time taken for cure, medical expenditure, duration and problems of living in and near polluting industries area, the nature of impact of pollution, preventive steps taken by the households and deaths in the family were collected through a questionnaire, using the direct personal interview method.

To analyse the growth of polluting Small Scale Industries in terms of number of units in Tamil Nadu and Madurai District, secondary data were required. A wider range of secondary data was collected from publications like Reports of Small Scale Industries Service Institute (SSISI), Small Scale Industries Hand Book of Statistics, Annual Report of Small Industries Development Corporation (SIDCO), Government of India, Economic Survey, Madras Institute of Development Studies (MIDS) Bulletin, Directory of Small Scale Industrial Units in Tamil Nadu, Records of District Industries Centre (DIC) and Tamil Nadu - An Economic Appraisal.

To a very great extent, the Researcher had to depend on the literatures related to the problem of study. A copy of the Interview Schedule used in the primary data collection has been added as Appendix (I, II and III).

SELECTION OF THE SAMPLE UNITS

The present study makes use of the sample survey method. Instead of obtaining data from all the units, which form the universe, sampling methods have been used. The sample is subjected to all processes of analysis and conclusions are drawn relating to the whole. Sample survey techniques employed, consist of diverse designs for securing representative samples.

There are totally 181 units, and 64 of them, which is 35 per cent sample size, have been chosen for study.

The proportional stratified random sampling technique is adopted in selecting the sample units. To have a considerable and reasonable number of units for study, the sample size has been fixed as 35 per cent. Accordingly, out of 98 chemical industry units, 35 have been chosen. In the case of cotton-dyeing industry, out of 54 units, 19 have been chosen. Out of 29 electroplating units, 10 have been chosen.

To assess the environmental impact of various polluting Small Scale Industries such as electroplating, cotton-dyeing, paint, soap and chemical manufacturing units on the industrial workers and households nearby situated, sixty-four workers and sixty-four households have been taken as sample respondents. The Researcher met the owners as well as the managers of the Small Scale Industrial Units to find out the names of workers who were actually involved in production and processing. The Researcher selected the sample workers from that list. The household, situated within one kilometre from the industrial unit, was selected as a sample item.

METHOD OF STUDY

This study covers sixty four small scale units, situated in Madurai District.

To analyse the growth rate of polluting Small Scale Industries in terms of number of units in Tamil Nadu and Madurai District, Compound Growth Rate by semi-log model was used. It covered eleven years from 1981-82 to 1991-92. Compound Growth Rate indicates the geometrical mean of annual growth rate. It is symbolically indicated as follows:

$$P_t = P_0 (1+r)^t$$
$$Y = a (1+r)^t$$
$$\log Y = \log a + t \log (1+r)$$
$$\log Y = a + bt$$

Where,

$$\alpha = \log a,$$
$$\beta = \log (1+r)$$

Compound Growth Rate = $r = e^b - 1$

$$r = e^b - 1 = (\text{Antilog } b) - 1$$

Water pollution in this study is measured in terms of BOD and COD. On the basis of results of the waste water analysis done in the Advanced Environmental Laboratory, Tamil Nadu Pollution Control Board, Pasumalai, Madurai, details of water pollution parameters are shown below.

Table 1
Water Pollution Parameters : Assessment

Industry	*Waste in Effluent*	*Actual Waste Load*
Electroplating	BOD	2293 mg/
	COD^5	2080 mg/l
Cotton-Dyeing		
1. Naphthol dyeing	BOD_5	298 mg/l
	COD	1600 mg/l
2. Vat dyeing	BOD_5	124 mg/l
	COD	620 mg/l
3. Direct dyeing	BOD_5	18 mg/l
	COD	144 mg/l

Source: Advanced Environmental Laboratory, Tamil Nadu Pollution Control Board, Pasumalai, Madurai.

In order to assess the impact of the quantity of waste water released, based on water pollution parameters namely

Biochemical Oxygen Demand (BOD) and Chemical Oxygen Demand (COD), a simple regression model has been fitted. It is a cross-sectional analysis for the year 1991-92.

The model estimated is

$$Y = a + bX$$

Where,

X stands for quantity of waste water in litres and
Y refers to the water pollution parameters in kilograms

(Therefore, Y = BOD or COD)

(a) is the value of BOD or COD (dependent variable) when the value of waste water (independent variable) is zero.

(b) is the marginal addition in water pollution parameters (dependent variable) when there is a unit addition in quantity of waste water (independent variable).

R^2 is defined as the ratio of the explained variance to the total variance. It is the co-efficient of determination and it measures the explaining capacity of the model.

$$\text{Co-efficient of Determination} = \frac{\text{Explained Variation}}{\text{Total Variation}}$$

the range of R^2 is from 0 to 1.

Air pollution is calculated on the basis of the type of fuel used. Here, in sample units there are two types of fuels used namely firewood and kerosene. Since only two units are using kerosene, this study concentrates on only firewood-based small units. The air pollution parameters are calculated on the basis of WHO's standards. According to the WHO's standards, one tonne of firewood is capable of generating air pollution load under different categories namely particulate matter, sulphurdioxide (SO_2), Oxides of Nitrogen (No_x), Hydrocarbons (Hc) and Carbon Monoxide (Co) as follows.

Table 2
Air Pollution Load Assessment

Sl. No.	*Air Pollution Load*	*Pollution Load per tonne of firewood in Kilograms*
1.	Particulates	13.700115
2.	Sulphurdioxide (SO_2)	20.100153
3.	Oxides of Nitrogen (NO_x)	2.7200077
4.	Hydrocarbons (Hc)	0.1400153
5.	Carbon Monoxide (Co)	0.7500191

Source: WHO 1992 Rapid Assessment, Sources of Air, Water and Land Pollution, No.62, Offset Publication, Geneva.

In the firewood-based Small Scale Units, air pollution load is calculated on the basis of the above WHO's standards.

A simple regression model is used to examine the influence of output on the air pollution load under different categories namely particulate matter, Sulphur dioxide (SO2), oxides of Nitrogen (NO), Hydrocarbons (HC) and carbon monoxide (CO) in cotton-dyeing and soap manufacturing units. It is a cross sectional analysis for the year 1991-92. The model is estimated

$$Y = a + bX$$

Where,

'X' refers to the output of cotton-dyeing or soap industry in kilograms,

'Y' stands for air pollution load under each category in kilograms.

'a' is the Y - intercept.

'b' is the marginal addition in air pollution load under each category when there is a unit addition in quantity of output.

Analysis of Variance is used in order to examine whether water pollution load and air pollution load vary in the three types of cotton-dyeing industries. It consists of classifying and cross-classifying statistical results and testing whether the means of a specified classification differs significantly. It refers to testing the significance of variance of parametric value within and between the groups.

$$F = \frac{\text{Between - Column Variance}}{\text{Within - Column Variance}}$$

Symbolically,

$$F = \frac{S_1^2}{S_2^2}$$

$$= \frac{SSC / c - 1}{SSE / n - c}$$

Where,

SSC = Sum of Squares between samples (Columns)

SSE = Sum of Squares within samples (rows)

c = Number of columns

n = Number of Items

If there is really a difference between the groups, the variance between the groups will be significantly larger than the variance within the groups.

To study the profile of polluting Small Scale Industries in Madurai District, three ratios are calculated - output-labour, output-capital and capital-labour ratios.

To identify the location and concentration of polluting Small Scale Industries in Madurai District, Sargant Florence's Inductive Approach is used. A descriptive analysis is used to assess the environmental impact of polluting Small Scale Industries on industrial workers and households residing nearby these polluting units and to review the existing controls and regulation measures of pollution control implemented by the Government of Tamil Nadu Pollution Control Board on Small Scale Industries.

OPERATIONAL DEFINITIONS OF TERMS AND CONCEPTS

Small Scale Industry

In March 1985, the Small Scale Industry was defined as an undertaking with a fixed capital investment of less than Rs.35

lakhs. As per the Industrial Policy Statement of May 1990, the investment ceiling in plant and machinery for Small Scale Industries was raised to Rs.60 lakhs. The present study is based on the definition of 1985, that is, industries having fixed capital investment of less than 35 lakhs.

Location and Concentration of Industry

Location of industry refers to the actual geographical position of an industry. Concentration of industries refers to the industries that are densely clustered in one region. Concentration of an industry leads to agglomeration. Location factor is calculated in order to find out the degree of location of a particular industry with the help of Sargant Florence's Inductive Approach.

Growth

The growth of an industry is defined as regular annual changes taking place in terms of one or more of the indicators such as employment, output, number of units, turnover or capital between the initial year and the terminal year. In the present study, growth is analysed in terms of growth rate of number of polluting small scale units in Tamil Nadu as well as in Madurai District.

Output-Capital Ratio (Capital Productivity)

Output-Capital Ratio expresses the relationship between the value of capital investment and the value of output. It refers to the number of units of output produced by one unit of capital. Both capital and output are expressed in rupees.

Output-Labour Ratio (Labour Productivity)

Output-Labour Ratio expresses the relationship between the number of labour and the value of output. It refers to the number of units of output produced by one unit of labour. Labour is expressed in numbers. Output is expressed in rupees.

Environmental Pollution

Environmental pollution may be defined as the unfavourable alteration of the surroundings, wholly or partially as a by-product of man's action, through direct or indirect effects of changes in energy use patterns, radiation levels, chemical and physical constitution and abundance of organisms. Environmental pollution in this study is confined to water pollution and air pollution.

Water Pollution

Water pollution is the process of altering the properties of any water rendering it unfit or less fit for the purpose. In this study, water pollution is measured by water pollution parameters namely Biochemical Oxygen Demand and Chemical Oxygen Demand.

Biochemical Oxygen Demand (BOD)

BOD is the dissolved oxygen required to decompose organic matter in water. It is a measure of pollution because the demand for oxygen increases when there is an increase in the effluents discharged into water. The amount of dissolved oxygen needed by decomposors to decompose organic materials in a given volume of water is called Biochemical Oxygen Demand (BOD).

Chemical Oxygen Demand (COD)

A measure of the oxygen required to oxidise all organic and inorganic compounds in water.

Air Pollution

Air pollution has been defined by World Health Organisation (WHO) as, "the presence in the air of substances put there by acts of man in concentrations sufficient to interfere with the comfort, safety, or health of man or with the full use or enjoyment of his property". The presence of contaminants in the atmosphere is considered to be in sufficient quantities and duration, to cause them to be injurious to human health, animal and plant life, and to reduce welfare in general. Air pollution is measured in terms of Particulates, Sulphur dioxide (SO_2), Oxides of Nitrogen (NOX), Hydrocarbons (HC) and Carbon Monoxide (Co) in this present study.

Environmental Impact

Environmental impact refers to any alteration of environmental conditions or the creation of a new set of environmental conditions, adverse or beneficial, caused or induced by the action or set of actions under consideration. The impact might be classified in terms of nuisance, economic or health effects. The environmental impact on factory workers and households who are living nearby the sample polluting Small Scale Industries are assessed in this study.

Occupational Disease

Occupational disease is that which arises out of or in the course of employment. In this study, occupational disease refers to the disease affecting the polluting small scale industrial workers.

4

Growth of Polluting Small Scale Industries– A Comparative Analysis of Sample Area

This chapter analyses the growth of the polluting Small Scale Industries in terms of number of units both in Tamil Nadu as well as Madurai District in particular. This chapter also examines the location and the concentration of the polluting Small Scale Industries in the sample area.

In a developing and predominantly agricultural economy like India's, Small Scale Industries can exercise a stabilising influence on the vagaries and uncertainties of rural economy, besides contributing to its prosperity. Apart from increased production, their development helps to serve as an important pillar in the country's industrial economy.

In the thirty-eight years after the launching of the Small Industries Movement in India in 1955, the small scale sector has developed considerably despite many odds. The growth in numbers of India's Small Scale Industries is from a mere 8.71 lakhs in 1980-81 to 22 lakhs in 1991-92.[1] The production of Small Scale Industries which was worth Rs.72,250 crores in 1986-87 has touched Rs.1,78,700 crores in 1991-92.[2] It has provided employment opportunities to 126.2 lakhs of persons in 1991-92. Further this sector has the distinction of earning foreign exchange to the tune of Rs.12,658 crores in the year 1991-92.[3]

While the industrial sector does contribute substantially to the national income, what is significant is that nearly a half of it comes from small scale units. The growth of industrial activity in any country is closely related to the progress of small industrial enterprises. The emphasis and efforts of the Government of India aim at promoting small scale units through fiscal incentives and appropriate policy measures.[4]

Tamil Nadu is counted among the industrially much advanced states in the country. It occupies the third place in the growth of industries next to Maharashtra and West Bengal. According to current estimates, the total number of registered units, belonging to different categories, is 1,27,202 with an annual production worth Rs.6,99,611 lakhs, besides an employment potential of 13.74 lakh people.[5]

In Madurai District, the industrial activities are mostly confined to the areas around Madurai, Thirumangalam and Theni. Nearly 85 per cent of the industries are located in these areas.[6] The number of registered Small Scale Industrial Units in Madurai District have increased from 1,303 in 1981-82 to 10,135 in 1991-92, nearly a growth of ten times.

Polluting Small Scale Industries have been growing in number both in Tamil Nadu as well as in Madurai District. These industries fall into four broad categories: Agro-based industries, Textile-based industries, Chemical-based industries and Engineering-based industries. An attempt has been made to examine the growth of these industries in the recent past on the basis of Tables 1 and 2.

For this purpose, a trend analysis is made with a model equation

$$Y = a + b\,t$$

'Y' refers to the number of producing units in a category of industries and 't' refers to the time period. The value of 'b' in this model is an average annual growth in the number of

Table 1
Industry-wise Classification Of Registered Ssi Units In Tamil Nadu

(in Numbers)

Sl. No.	*Industry Group*	*Years* 1982	1984	1985	1986	1987	1988	1991
1.	Agro-based Industries	4725	7522	9790	10506	11969	13277	19722
2.	Textile-based Industries	4830	7639	9458	9896	11270	13157	22084
3.	Chemical-based Industries	9749	11749	13244	13709	15597	17001	23209
4.	Engineering & Allied based Industries	10634	14018	17708	18714	21319	23278	31218
	Total	29938	40928	50200	52825	60155	66713	96233

Source: Small Industries Service Institute, Ministry of India, Government of India, Madras

Table 2
Trends In Number of Units of Polluting Small Scale Industries In Madurai District

(in Numbers)

		Names of Categories				
Sl. No.	*Year*	*Agro-based industries*	*Textile-based industries*	*Chemical-based industries*	*Engineer-ing- based industries*	*Total*
1.	1981-82	244	75	168	398	885
2.	1982-83	322	90	186	431	1029
3.	1983-84	360	93	216	480	1149
4.	1984-85	448	129	258	625	1460
5.	1985-86	526	188	309	798	1821
6.	1986-87	654	199	397	956	2206
7.	1987-88	754	227	501	1162	2644
8.	1988-89	837	247	549	1300	2933
9.	1989-90	924	306	629	1442	3301
10.	1990-91	1023	369	709	1536	3637
11.	1991-92	1149	989	814	1666	4618

Source: District Industries Centre, Madurai

units. The compound growth rate at which these industries have grown has also been worked out by the estimating model

$$\text{Log } Y = \alpha + \beta t$$

The compound growth 'g' is worked out as

$$g = (\text{Antilog } \beta\text{-}1) \times 100$$

The growth rate of the polluting Small Scale Industries in Tamil Nadu has been estimated and presented in Table 3.

Table 3

Growth Rate of The Polluting Small Scale Industries In Tamil Nadu (From 1982 To 1991)

Model : Y = a + b t

Sl. No.	*Name of the Industries*	*a*	*b*	*R^2*	*F*	*Compound growth @ rate %*
1.	Agro-based Industries	2747.90* (524.27)	168.77** (90.29)	0.9847	321.42	16.38
2.	Textile-based Industries	1810.61 (1213.65)	1823.88** (209.02)	0.9384	76.14	17.31
3.	Chemical-based Industries	7308.52** (721.14)	1474.96** (124.20)	0.9658	141.04	10.01
4.	Engineering-based Industries	7812.15** (538.14)	2283.44** (92.68)	0.9918	607.01	12.58
5.	All Polluting Industries	19676.17* (2822.27)	7201.05** (486.06)	0.9777	219.49	13.45

Source: Small Scale Industries Service Institute, Madras.

Note: * Significant at 5% level

** Significant at 1% level

(Figures in brackets refer to the Standard Error)

@ Estimated with the semi-log model.

The average growth rate in all categories is quite considerable and significant at 1 per cent level.

AGRO-BASED INDUSTRIES

In the Agro-based industries, R^2 value is 0.9847 which indicates that the model explains more than 98 per cent of variation in the growth of the units. The average growth is more than 1600 units annually. The compound growth rate in these industries is 16.38 per cent.

TEXTILE-BASED INDUSTRIES

In the Textile-based industries the co-efficient of determination is 0.9384 which implies that 93 per cent of variation in the dependent variable is explained by the model. The average growth is more than 1800 units per annum. The compound growth rate in these industries is 17.31 per cent.

CHEMICAL-BASED INDUSTRIES

In the chemical-based industries the co-efficient of determination is equal to 0.9658 which implies that the model is able to explain 96 per cent of variation of the dependent variable, that is, number of units. The average growth is nearer to 1500 units per annum. The compound growth rate in these industries is 10.01 per cent.

ENGINEERING-BASED INDUSTRIES

In the engineering-based industries R2 value is 0.9777 which would mean that 97 per cent of the variation in the dependent variable, that is, number of units have been explained by the independent variable, that is, time in years. The average growth is nearer to 2300 units annually. The compound growth rate in these industries is 12.58 per cent.

Of all the polluting Small Scale Industries in Tamil Nadu, the compound growth rate of the textile-based industries is the highest (17.31 per cent). Next to that are the agro-based industries, which have the second highest compound growth rate (16.38 per cent). The compound growth rate of the engineering-based industries occupies the third place (12.58 per cent). Chemical-based industries are in the fourth place (10.01 per cent). The compound growth rate of all the polluting industries in Tamil Nadu is estimated to be 13.45 per cent.

The growth rate of the polluting Small Scale Industries in Madurai District has been calculated and presented in Table 4. The average growth rate in all categories is quite considerable and significant at 1 per cent level.

Table 4
Growth Rate Of The Polluting Small Scale Industries In Madurai District (From 1982 To 1991)
Model : Y = A + Bt

Sl. No.	*Name of the Industries*	*a*	*b*	R^2	*F*	*Compound growth @ rate %*
1.	Agro-based Industries	111.35** (17.97)	91.16** (02.65)	0.9925	11.84	16.51
2.	Textile-based Industries	-95.27 (111.49)	60.00** (16.44)	0.5968	11.32	23.93
3.	Chemical-based Industries	30.46 (25.76)	66.68** (3.80)	0.9716	308.36	18.25
4.	Engineering-based Industries	143.46** (39.58)	139.64** (5.84)	0.9845	572.50	17.12
5.	All Polluting Industries	189.98 (152.15)	357.42** (22.43)	0.9658	253.94	18.04

Source: District Industries Centre, Madras

Note: * Significant at 5% level

** Significant at 1% level

(Figures in brackets refer to the Standard Error)

@ Estimated with the semi-log model.

AGRO-BASED INDUSTRIES

In the Agro-based industries, R^2 value is 0.9925 which indicates that the model explains 99 per cent of variation in the number of the units. The average growth is more than 91 units annually. The compound growth rate in these industries is 16.51 per cent.

TEXTILE-BASED INDUSTRIES

In the textile-based industries, the co-efficient of determination is 0.5968 which would mean that 59 per cent of variation in the dependent variable is explained by the model. The average growth has been equal to 90 units per annum. The compound growth rate in these industries is 23.93 per cent.

CHEMICAL-BASED INDUSTRIES

In the chemical-based industries R^2 is equal to 0.9716 which denotes that 97 per cent of the variation in the dependent variable that is, the number of the units has been explained by the independent variable that is, time in years. The average growth is more than 66 units per annum. The compound growth rate in these industries is 18.25 per cent.

ENGINEERING-BASED INDUSTRIES

In the engineering-based industries, the co-efficient of determination is 0.9845 which implies that 98 per cent of variation in the dependent variable is explained by the model. The average growth has been more than 130 units annually. The compound growth rate in these industries is 17.12 per cent.

Of all the polluting Small Scale Industries in Madurai District, the compound growth rate of the textile- based industries is the highest (23.93 per cent). Next come the chemical-based industries which have the second highest compound growth rate (18.25 per cent). The compound growth rate of the engineering-based industries occupies the thrid place (17.12 per cent). Agro-based industries are in the fourth place (16.51 per cent). The compound growth rate of all the polluting industries in Madurai District is estimated to be approximately 18.04 per cent.

The compound growth rate of the agro-based industries in Tamil nadu is 16.38 per cent whereas it is 16.51 per cent in Madurai District. Both are more or less the same.

The compound growth rate of the textile-based industries in Tamil Nadu is 17.31 per cent. It is less than that of Madurai District. The compound growth rate of the textile-based industries in Madurai District is 23.93 per cent.

The compound growth rate of the chemical-based industries in Tamil Nadu and Madurai District are 10.01 per cent and 18.25 per cent respectively. It is evident that the chemical-based industries of Madurai District have more compound growth rate than that of Tamil Nadu.

Engineering-based industries in Tamil Nadu and Madurai District have the compound growth rate of 12.58 per cent and 17.12 per cent respectively, which means that the compound growth rate of Madurai District is higher than that of Tamil Nadu as for as the engineering-based industries are concerned.

Table 5

Polluting Small Scale Industries In Madurai District And Tamil Nadu

(in Numbers)

		Names of Categories				
		Agro-based industries	*Textile-based industries*	*Chemical-based industries*	*Engineering-based industries*	*Total*
1982	Tamil Nadu	4725	4830	9749	10634	29938
	Madurai District	322	90	186	431	1029
1991	Tamil Nadu	19722	22084	23209	21218	96233
	Madurai District	1149	989	814	1666	4618
1982	Madurai District (in per-centage)	6.82	1.86	1.91	4.05	3.44
1991		5.83	4.48	3.50	5.34	4.80

Sources: 1 Small Industries Service Institute, Ministry of India, Government of India, Madras.

2 District Industries Centre, Madurai.

The compound growth rate of all the polluting industries in Tamil Nadu is only 13.45 per cent. It is less than that of Madurai District which is 18.04 per cent. The role of polluting Small Scale Industries in Madurai District with reference to Tamil Nadu as a whole, is presented in Table 5.

Among the entire polluting Small Scale Industries in Tamil Nadu, in the year 1982, 6.82 per cent of the agro-based industries, 1.86 per cent of the textile-based industries, 1.91 per cent of the chemical-based industries and 4.05 per cent of the engineering-based industries are located in Madurai District. Among them the engineering-based industries are the highest in number (431) and the textile-based industries are the lowest in number (90) situated in Madurai District. Totally 3.44 per cent of the polluting Small Scale Industries of the entire Tamil Nadu in 1982 were situated in Madurai District.

Among the entire polluting Small Scale Industries in Tamil Nadu in the year 1991, 5.83 per cent of the agro-based industries, 4.48 per cent of the textile-based industries, 3.5 per cent of the chemical-based industries and 5.34 per cent of the engineering-based industries are located in Madurai District. Among them the engineering-based industries are the highest in number (1666) and the chemical-based industries are the lowest in number (84) situated in Madurai District. Totally 4.8 per cent of the polluting Small Scale Industries of the entire Tamil Nadu in 1991 were located in Madurai District.

In between 1982 and 1991, the contribution of agro-based industries in Madurai District to Tamil Nadu has decreased from 6.82 per cent to 5.83 per cent. The textile-based industries in Madurai District has increased its contribution to Tamil Nadu from 1.86 per cent to 4.48 per cent, chemical-based industries has increased its contribution from 1.9 per cent to 3.5 per cent, and engineering-based industries has also increased its contribution from 4.05 per cent to 5.34 per cent. Totally all the polluting industries have increased their contribution from 3.44 per cent to 4.8 per cent.

The following four pie diagrams are drawn based on the details given in Table 5.

Among the polluting industries in Tamil Nadu, engineering-based industries, in 1982, occupy the predominant position of 36 per cent of the total. (Figure 1). This position continued in 1991 also, as it was 32 per cent of the total (Figure 2). Chemical-based industries occupy the second position in both the years 1982 and 1991. Other industries (textile-based and agro-based industries) occupy the third and the fourth positions respectively.

Figure 1
The Role of Polluting Small Scale Industries – 1982

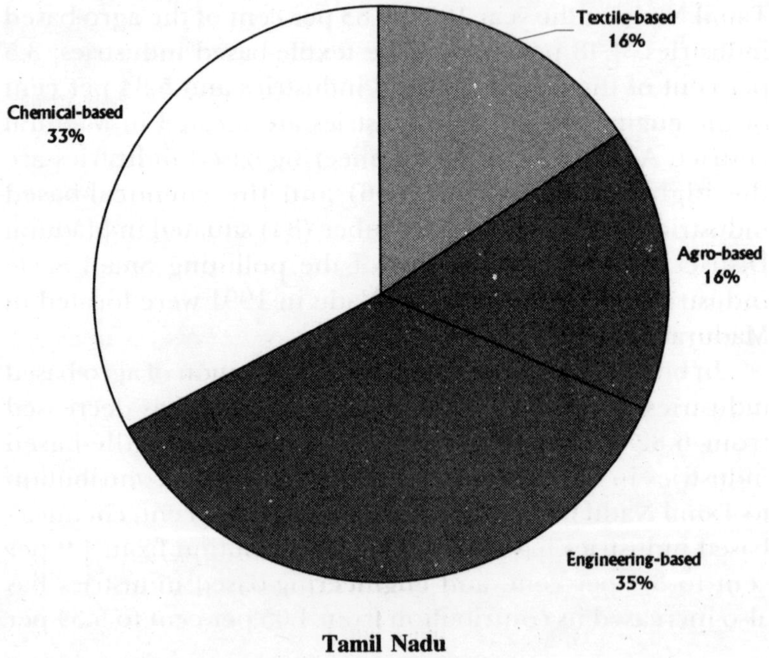

Tamil Nadu

Figure 2

The Role of Polluting Small Scale Industries – 1991

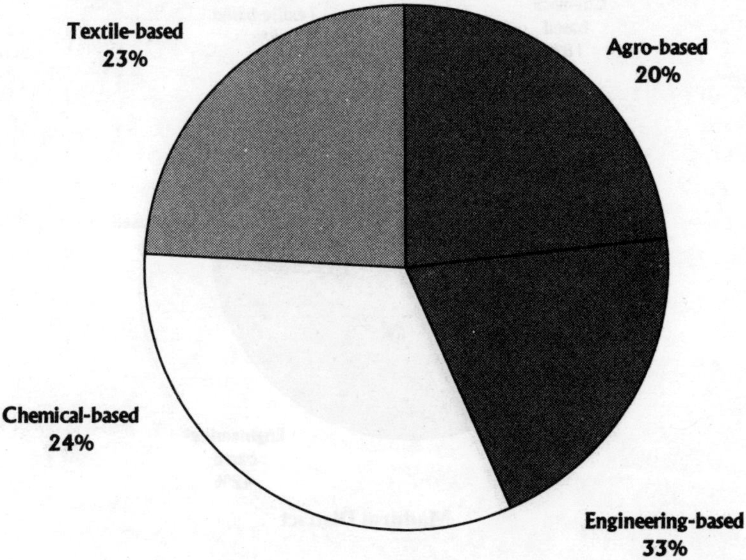

Tamil Nadu

Among the polluting industries in Madurai District, engineering-based industries occupy, in 1982, the predominant position of 42 per cent of the total (Figure 3). This position continued in 1991 also, as its position was 36 per cent of the total (Figure 4). Agro-based industries occupy the second position in both the years 1982 and 1991. In 1982 chemical-based industries occupy the third place while they are in the fourth place in 1991. In 1982, textile-based industries occupy the fourth place while they are in the third place in 1991.

The above analysis indicates that the polluting Small Scale Industries are increasing both in Tamil Nadu and Madurai District.

Figure 3
The Role of Polluting Small Scale Industries – 1982

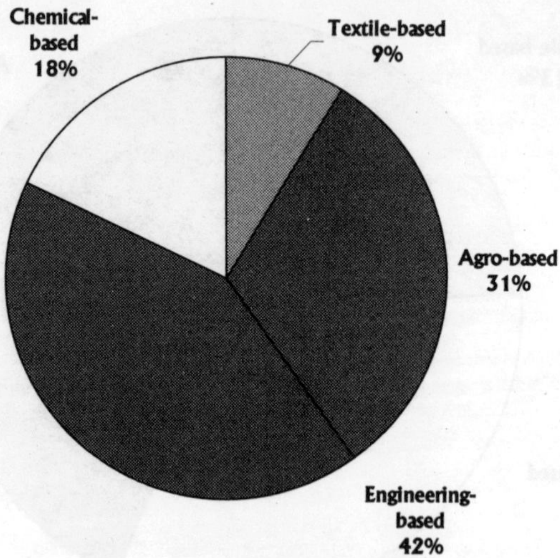

Madurai District

Figure 4
The Role Of Polluting
Small Scale Industries – 1991

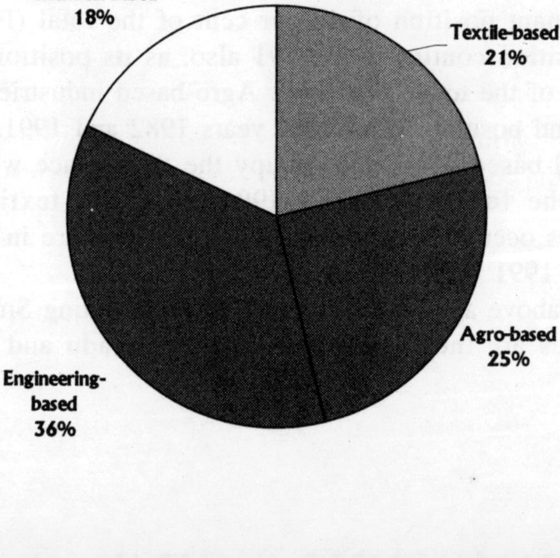

LOCATION AND CONCENTRATION OF POLLUTING SMALL SCALE INDUSTRIAL UNITS IN MADURAI DISTRICT

The term 'Location of industry' refers to the actual geographical position of an industry or firm within the industry. The study of specific industries reveals wide variations in their distribution patterns.[7] The choice of industrial location changes the level of efficiency for industrial undertakings. For an industrial undertaking to operate profitably, it must have easy access to raw materials, labour, power and markets. It was only after the introduction of the factory system that the problem of industrial location became all the more important.[8] According to Weber, the location of manufacturing industries is determined by the ratio between the weight of localized material and the weight of the product. This ratio, Weber calls the 'Material Index'. Higher the material index, the greater will be the degree of concentration of industries at the centre of consumption. For example, Indian textile, jute and iron and steel industries, despite the development of transport were very much influenced by the nearness of sources of raw materials.

The most dominant consideration for locating an industrial unit at a particular place, always is to secure the maximum efficiency of production and distribution.[9] The theory of industrial location has been developed mainly to achieve this purpose.

LOCATION THEORY

The contribution of the classical economists to the theory of industrial location is meagre. Location Theories help us to understand the pre-requisites which are considered to be important and necessary for a profit maximising firm to locate its plant in any particular region or particular location.

But in recent years, location theory has been extended beyond the classical free market paradigm of profit maximisation of firm. Location theory is being utilised for regional development planning. In this context it is worthnoting what William Alonso says, "Increasingly the question of location of a factory is being considered as 'project' by a Government agency rather than as a profit-making venture by a private corporation. In this case, theory of location of the firm extends to project planning but antecedes regional and national planning". Industrial location can, therefore, be considered an important aspect of industrial development in a backward region.[10]

Weber's Theory of Location (Least Cost Approach)

It was Alfred Weber who, for the first time, attempted an analytical approach to the problem of location for manufacturing industries.

The method of treatment adopted is purely deductive. According to Weber, certain technical co-efficient plays a major and decisive role in determining the location of an industry. He maintained that the choice of place for the location of an industry is decided by three principal costs, namely, transport cost, labour cost and cost due to excessive agglomeration.

Industries with high manufacturing cost in the total cost of production also tend to concentrate, more so, if labour costs form a large proportion of its manufacturing cost. This tendency to concentrate is known as the, 'co-efficient of manufacture per locational ton'. Industries with high co-efficient of manufacture have strong tendency to concentrate.[11]

His theory has been criticised for his unrealistic approach and deductive reasoning. Industrial location cannot be explained by mere theoretical generalizations and unreal assumptions. He has omitted entrepreneurial ability or capital availability.

'Demand or Locational Interdependence Approach' by August Losch deals with demand as the major spatial variable. According to this theory, demand varies from place to place and market for the product is scattered. He based his model on three fundamental factors, namely existence of space exploiting activities, transportation costs and economies of scale. He says that the right approach is to find the place of maximum profits, where total revenue exceeds total cost by the greatest amount. He stressed the importance of the accessibility to the maximum share of the market in deciding upon the location.

'The Integrated or Profit Maximisation Theory' by Melvin Greenhut aims at integrating the Least Cost Approach (Weber) and Demand Approach (Losch). He believes that transportation cost will be the determining factor in industrial location only when the cost of transportation forms a substantial part of the total cost. In this case, production will be located nearer the market or source of raw materials. Nature of product, size of the unit and degree of elasticity can also be the factors in deciding the location.[12] It takes note of both institutional and non-institutional factors and therefore is a useful general statement of industrial location.

'Inductive Analysis' by Sargant Florence deals with the transportation cost as an important location factor. He observes "the relation of an industry to an area is not so important as the relation of the industry to the distribution of the occupied population as a whole". He has introduced two new concepts in the terminology of the theory of industrial location, namely, 'Location Quotient' and 'Co-efficient of Localization'.[13]

They are used for measuring the statistical determination of the degree of location.

Location Quotient is an index of the degree of concentration of an industry in a particular place. The index is arrived at by taking the percentage of all workers in a particular industry found in a certain region and dividing it by the proportion in that particular region of the total industrial workers in the country.[14] If the locational quotient is close to the unity for each region, the industry will be evenly scattered over the whole country, whereas if the industry is localized in any particular region, the location quotient will be more than unity for the region.[15] On the other hand, if it is below unity, the region is not supposed to have a sufficient share of the industry.

The Co-efficient of localization is indicative of the propensity of each industry for concentration. It can be worked out for an industry from the census of production data by the following formula: "When the workers are divided up region by region as percentages of the total in all regions, the co-efficient is the sum (divided by 100) of the plus deviations of the regional percentages of workers in the particular industry from the corresponding regional percentages of workers in all industry".[16] Industries with a low co-efficient of localization can thrive in different regions and are dispersed, whereas industries which show a high co-efficient of localization are concentrated in particular regions. The indices provided by Sargant Florence are of greater help in studying the locational dynamics in any country.

LOCATIONAL PECULIARITY

With the Small Scale Industries, there is great locational rigidity in the sense that these industries are attached to certain localities. Many of these industries are located where the skilled workers or working population, in general, are available and not at the places where the products in question are needed or the raw materials are available. The places with plentiful labour supply exercise a pull on the location of these industries. This makes the Small Scale Industries particularly amenable to dispersal, for in a country like India, population is most widely dispersed.[17]

This shift in locational bias influences the cost structure of these industries favourably. The cost of labour is the most significant of all costs of production and many Small Scale Industries are located at places of plentiful labour supply. Whenever there is some choice as between alternative locations it is over-weighed by the availability of labour.

Though the location of these industries is influenced by the factor of plentiful labour supply, there are other factors too, like marketing costs and production costs which may influence the location of these industries. In the case of both internal and external economies Small Scale Industries are in a disadvantageous position. Due to their small size, internal economies are not available for them and external economies cannot be enjoyed by them because of their wide dispersal or wide spread location.[18]

If the Small Scale Industries are located or concentrated nearer to one another, they may achieve external economies like common marketing facilities, promotion of skilled labour and common technical services. As small units accounting for small quantities of output in the total output of the industry concerned, their influence on the total supply is not significant and their inclination to join into a combination is meagre.[19]

On the inductive side, Sargant Florence offers a different analysis which has assumed great practical significance during recent years. The location quotient gives the degrees of concentration of a particular industry in a particular region. Location quotient can be computed by two different methods. (i) By dividing (a) the percentage share of the region in the total workers employed in the industry by (b) the percentage share of the region in the total working population, and (ii) by dividing (a) the percentage share of the industry in the total workers employed in the region by (b) the percentage share of the industry in the total working population.

Both these methods, according to him, yield the same result. If location quotient is close to unity for each region, the industry will be evenly scattered over the whole country, whereas if the industry is localized in any particular region, the location quotient will be more than unity for region and zero or so for others.

The location quotient is used in this study in order to measure the degree of concentration of the Small Scale

Industries, namely cotton-based industry, chemical industry and electroplating industry in Madurai District.

In Table 6, the details regarding the total number of workers in cotton-based industries, chemical industry and electroplating industry in Madurai District are given.

In Table 7, the details regarding the total number of workers in all types of Small Scale Industries in Madurai District are given.

Table 6

Industrial Workers' Distribution In Polluting Small Scale Industries In Madurai District (1991-92)

Sl. No.	*Name of the Taluk*	*Workers In Numbers*			
		Cotton-Based Industries	*Chemical Industry*	*Electro-Plating Industry*	*Total*
1.	Usilampatti	—	3	—	3
2.	Andipatti	93	—	—	93
3.	Uthamapalayam	22	39	—	61
4.	Aadipatti	9	36	—	45
5.	Madurai South	1621	774	177	2572
6.	Madurai North	129	186	14	329
7.	Melur	—	26	—	26
8.	Periyakulam	1103	44	4	1151
9.	Thirumangalam	221	79	—	300
	Total (Madurai District)	3198	1187	195	4580

Sources: 1. Directory of Small Scale Industrial Units In Tamil Nadu.
2. District Industries Centre, Madurai.

Based on Tables 6 and 7, the location factors for cotton-based industries, chemical industry and electroplating industry in Madurai District are calculated and the findings are given below

Table 7

Total Numbei of Small Scale Industrial Workers In Madurai District (1991-92)

Sl. No.	*Name of the Taluk*	*Total Workers in all types of Small Scale Industries*
1.	Usilampatti	1526
2.	Andipatti	1486
3.	Uthamapalayam	2751
4.	Vadipatti	1057
5.	Madurai South	31003
6.	Madurai North	9187
7.	Melur	1395
8.	Periyakulam	5496
9.	Thirumangalam	3815
	Total (Madurai District)	57716

Sources: 1. Directory of Small Scale Industrial Units In Tamil Nadu.
2. District Industries Centre, Madurai.

Total number of workers employed in all industries in the country = X. Total number of workers employed in particular industry = X1. Total number of workers in particular region = Y. Total number of workers employed in particular industry in that region = Y1.

A. Percentage of workers in particular industry to all workers in that industry in particular region

$$= \frac{Y_1 \times 100}{X_1}$$

B. Percentage of workers in particular region to total industrial workers in the country.

$$= \frac{Y \times 100}{X}$$

Location Factor = A/B.

Location Factor of polluting Small Scale Industries in Madurai District is given in Table 8.

The computation details of the location quotient for the cotton-based industries, chemical industry and electroplating industry in Madurai District are given in Appendix A. 1.

Table 8

Location Factor of Polluting Small Scale Industries In Madurai District

Sl. No.	*Name of The Taluk*	*Location Factor*		
		Cotton-based Industries	*Chemical Industry*	*Electro- Plating Industry*
1.	Usilampatti	—	0.10	—
2.	Andipatti	1.13	—	—
3.	Uthamapalayam	0.14	0.69	—
4.	Vadipatti	0.15	1.66	—
5.	Madurai South	0.94	1.21	1.69
6.	Madurai North	0.25	0.98	0.45
7.	Melur	—	0.91	—
8.	Periyakulam	3.62	0.39	0.22
9.	Thirumangalam	1.05	1.01	—

Source: Computed Data

From Table 8 it is clear that as for as the cotton-based industries are concerned, units are not evenly distributed over the taluks. It is found that Periyakulam Taluk has the largest concentration of units with the location quotient of 3.62. Next comes Andipatti Taluk with the location quotient of 1.13. The location quotients of Thirumangalam Taluk and Madurai South Taluk are 1.05 and 0.94 respectively indicating the average level of concentration. The other taluks, namely Uthamapalayam, Vadipatti and Madurai North have low values of location quotient showing a sparse distribution of units.

From Table 8 it is obvious that in the case of chemical industry in Madurai District, units are not evenly distributed over the taluks. It is observed that Vadipatti Taluk has the largest concentration of units with the location quotient of 1.66. Next comes Madurai South Taluk with the location quotient of 1.21. The location quotients of Madurai North Taluk, Melur Taluk and Thirumangalam Taluk are 0.98, 0.91 and 1.01 respectively. The other three taluks, namely Usilampatti, Uthamapalayam and Periyakulam have low values of location quotient which is below unity showing that the above three taluks are not supposed to have a sufficient share of the chemical industry.

It could be inferred from the above table that the electroplating industry is not equally distributed over the taluks. It is clear that Madurai South Taluk has the largest concentration of units with the location quotient of 1.69. The other two taluks namely Madurai North and Periyakulam have low values of location quotient showing that there is a sparse distribution of units.

In Madurai South Taluk, electroplating industry has more concentration than chemical and cotton-based industries. Chemical industry also has above normal level of concentration. Cotton-based industries have the below normal level of concentration. In Periyakulam Taluk it is found that cotton-based industries have greater concentration. Chemical and electroplating industries have below average level of concentration. In Madurai North Taluk, Chemical industry has normal level of concentration. Cotton-based and electroplating industries have below normal level of concentration.

In Thirumangalam Taluk, it is found that cotton- based and chemical industries have average level of concentration. In Vadipatti Taluk, chemical industry has greater concentration and cotton-based industries have below average level of concentration. In Uthampalayam Taluk both cotton-based and chemical industries have below average level of concentration.

Thus considering the location quotient of the three industries in all the nine taluks, it is found that only Madurai South Taluk has concentration of all the three industries, either at the average level or at a greater level. This implies that Madurai South Taluk ranks first in the industrial activities of Madurai District.

Industrial units in the Madurai South Taluk are flourishing because of the following reasons. Apart from the concession given in the electricity charges, conveyance facilities to bring the raw materials from outside and to carry the finished products to the outside markets are also available. Water facilities, particularly both corporation water and borewell water, are available quite sufficiently. When interviewed for data the factory owners said Madurai South Taluk was in the centre of the town and the availability of labourers was also quite satisfactory. Besides, 53.72 per cent of the total number of workers in the whole of Madurai District were available in Madurai South Taluk. This is evident from Table 8.

LOCATION OF POLLUTING SMALL SCALE INDUSTRIES IN MADURAI DISTRICT

Madurai District comprises nine taluks namely Andipatti, Madurai North, Madurai South, Melur, Periyakulam, Vadipatti, Thirumangalam, Uthamapalayam and Usilampatti. Recently Peraiyur became one of the taluks of the Madurai District. The Small Scale Industries that are located in nine taluks during the study period are shown in Map 1.

Among the Small Scale Industries, the polluting industries are soap, paint, chemical, electroplating and cotton-dyeing units. Their location is shown in the above map. From the map, it is clear that more polluting units are concentrated in three taluks namely Thirumangalam, Madurai South and Madurai North.

Small Scale Industries are greatly attracted to function within the Corporation limits. This is clear from the Madurai

Map 1

Location of Polluting Smalle Scale Industries in Madurai District

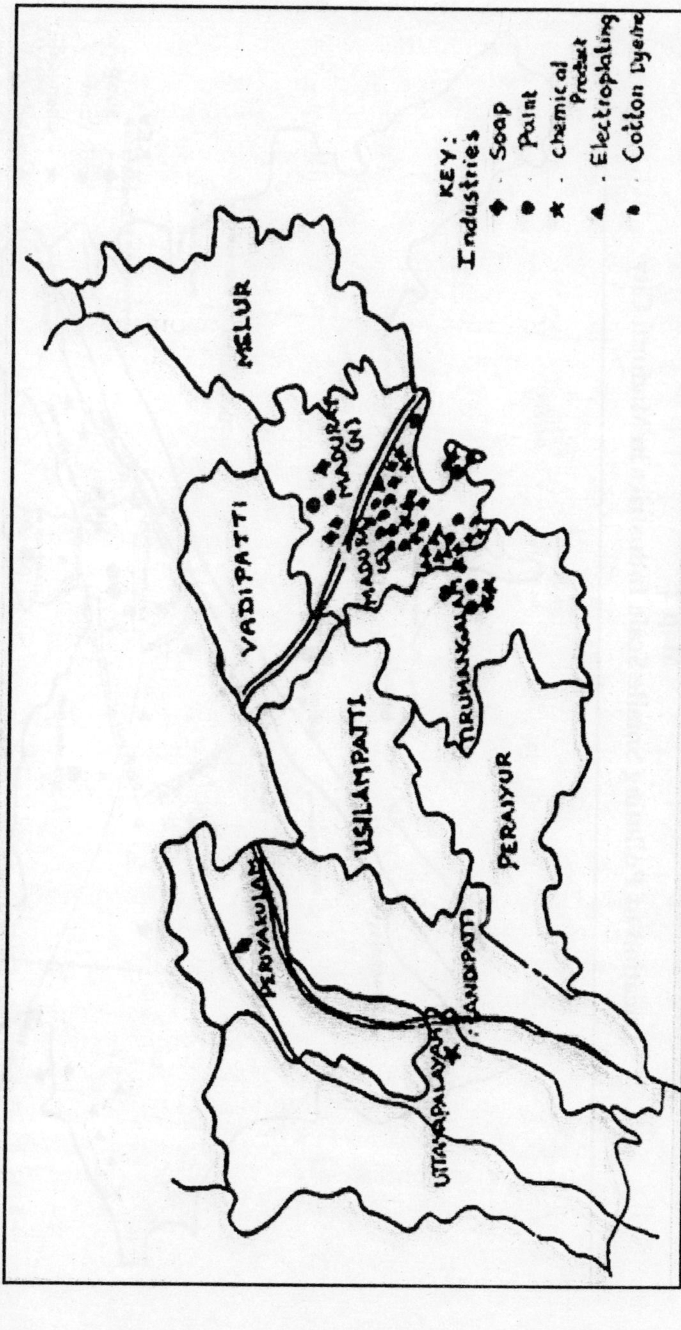

Map 2

Location of Polluting Smalle Scale Industries in Madurai City

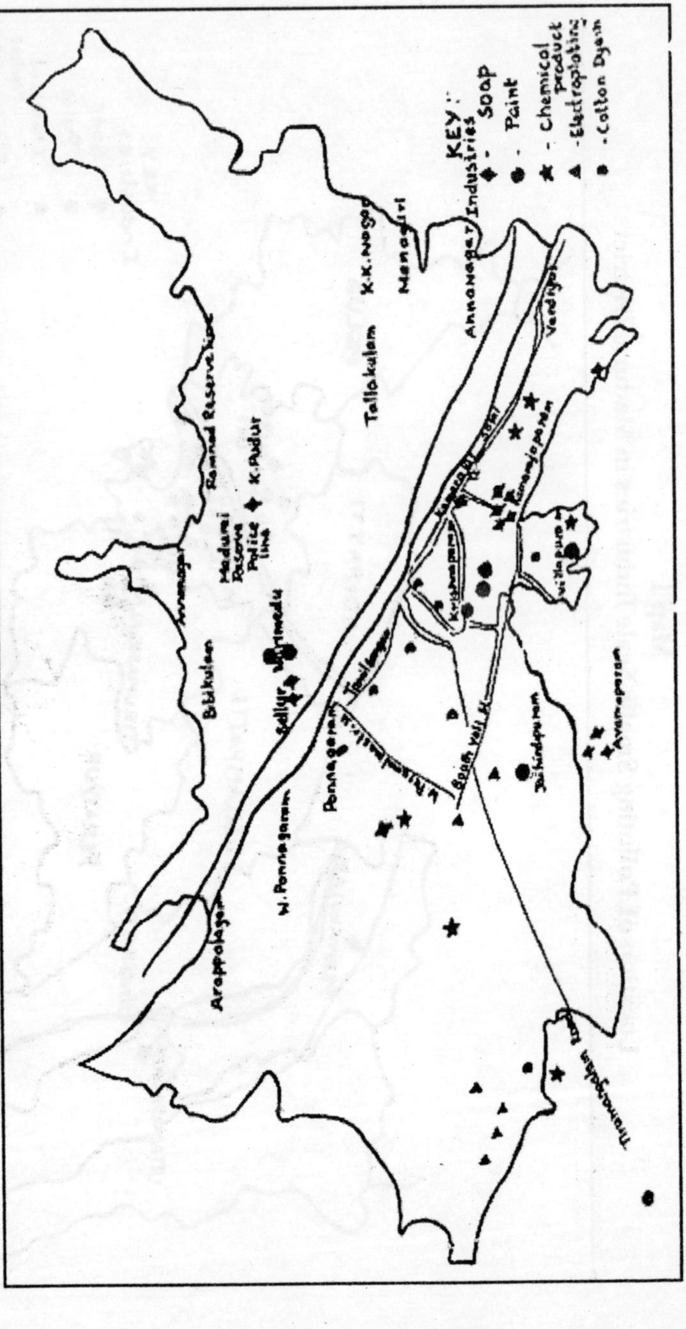

Map 3
Location of Soap Industry in Madurai District

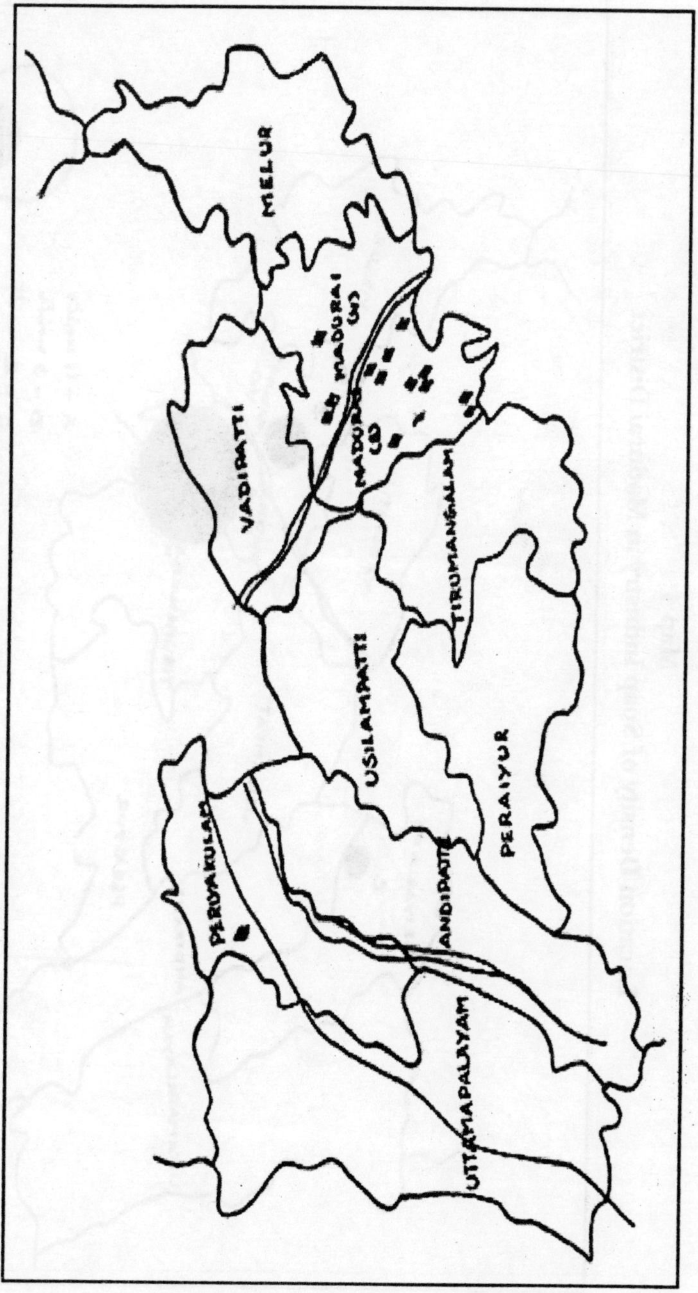

Map 4
Location Density of Soap Industry in Madurai District

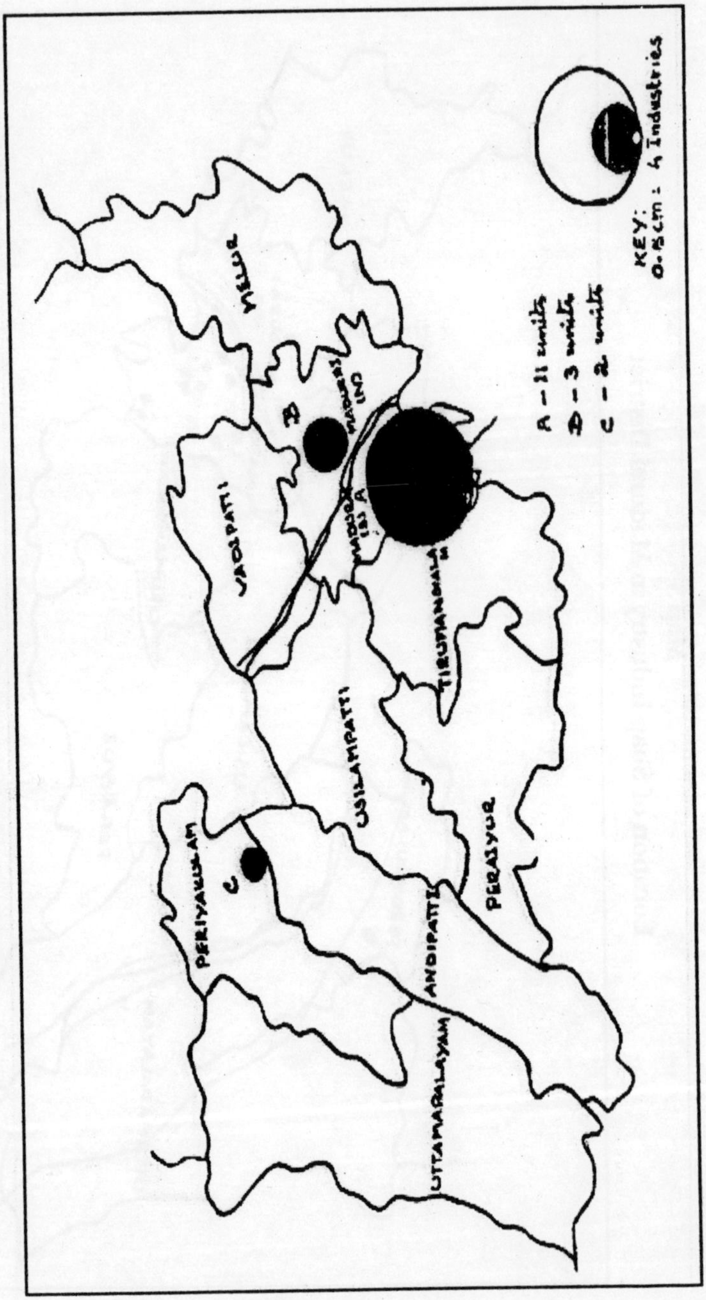

city Map, attached (Map 2). Most of the polluting Small Scale Industries are situated in and around Madurai City.

SOAP MANUFACTURING INDUSTRY

While analysing the locations of the soap manufacturing industry (Map 3) it is found that nearly eleven units are situated in Madurai South Taluk, three units in Madurai North and two units in Periyakulam Taluk. No other taluk has soap units.

The Density of the soap industries' location is shown in Map 4.

PAINT INDUSTRY

The polluting paint industry is located in three taluks namely Thirumangalam, Madurai South and Madurai North. The number of units in Thirumangalam Taluk is five. In Madurai North and Madurai South, it is two and four respectively (Map 5).

The degree of concentration of these industry is shown in Map 6 and it is proportionate to the size of the circle.

CHEMICAL PRODUCT INDUSTRY

The polluting chemical product industry is located in three taluks namely Madurai South, Thirumangalam and Uthamapalayam. The number of units in Thirumangalam, Madurai South and Uthamapalayam are three, seven and one respectively (Map 7).

The location density of the chemical product industry is shown in Map 8.

ELECTROPLATING INDUSTRY

While analysing the location of electroplating industry it is found that ten units are located in Madurai South Taluk only. It is shown in Map 9.

The location density of the electroplating industry is shown in Map 10.

Map 5
Location of Paint Industry in Madurai District

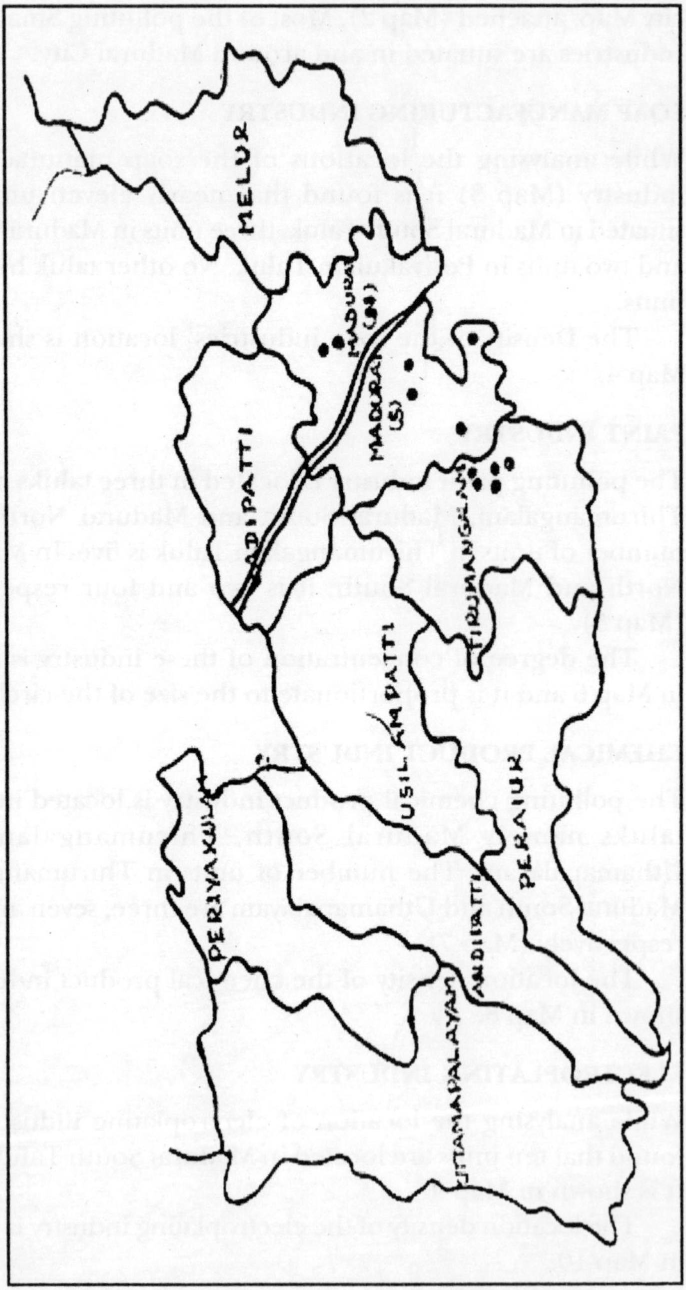

Map 6

Location Density of Paint Industry in Madurai District

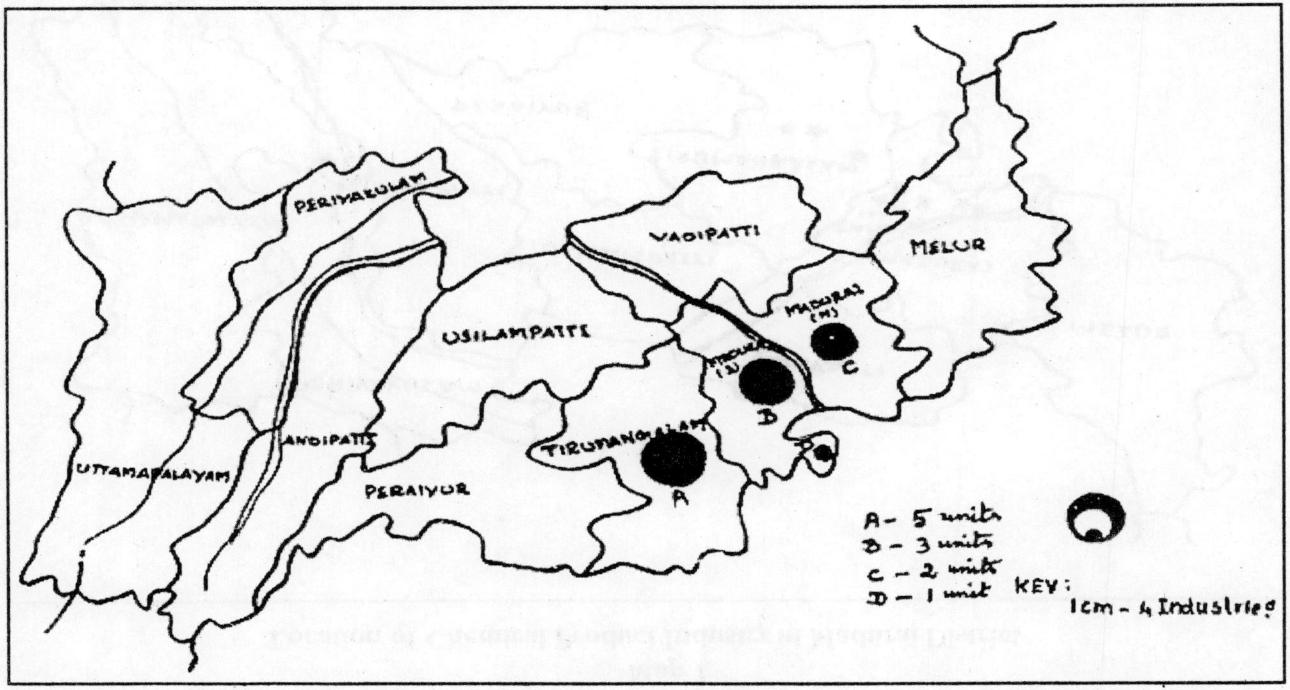

Map 7
Location of Chemical Product Industry in Madurai District

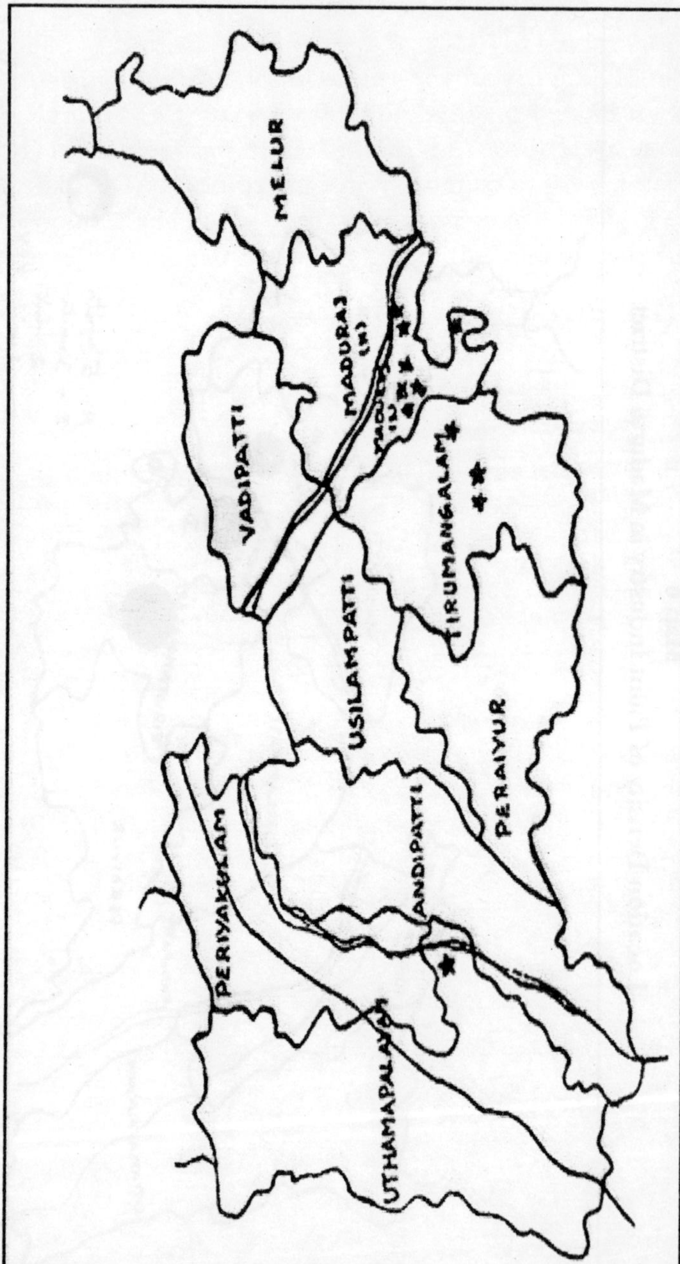

Map 8

Location of Chemical Product Industry in Madurai District

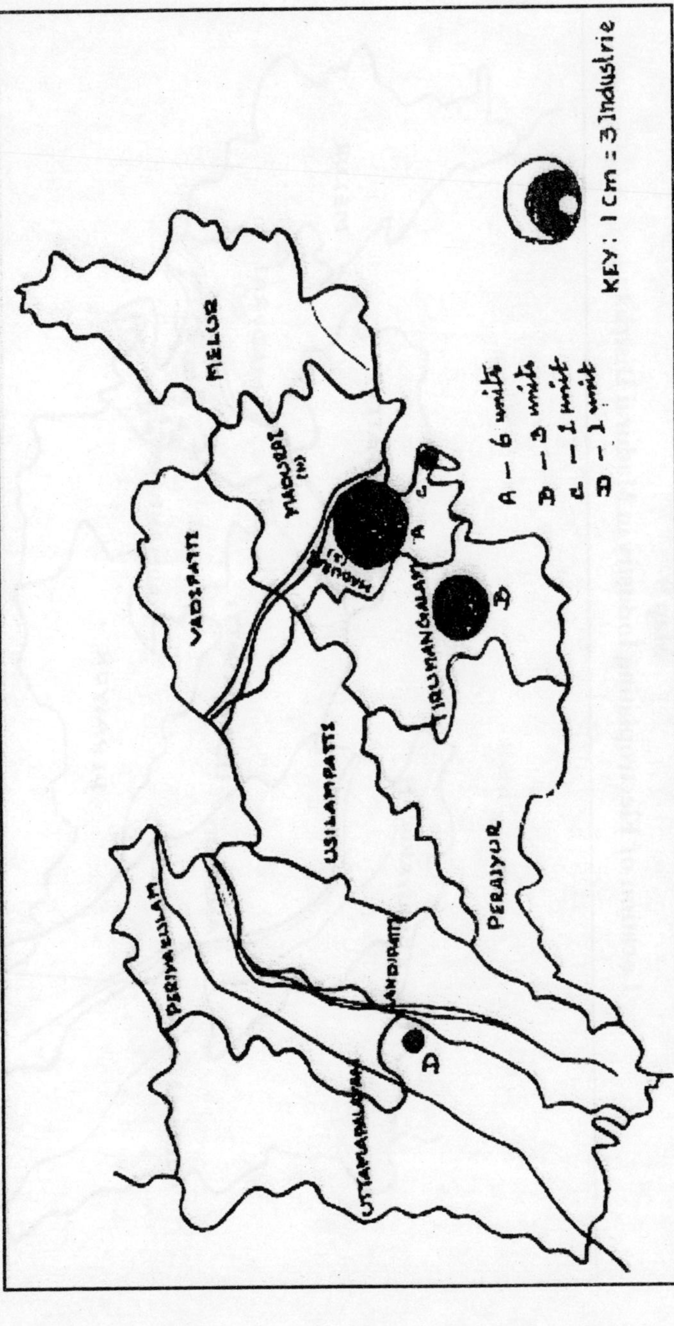

Map 9

Location of Electroplating Industry in Madurai District

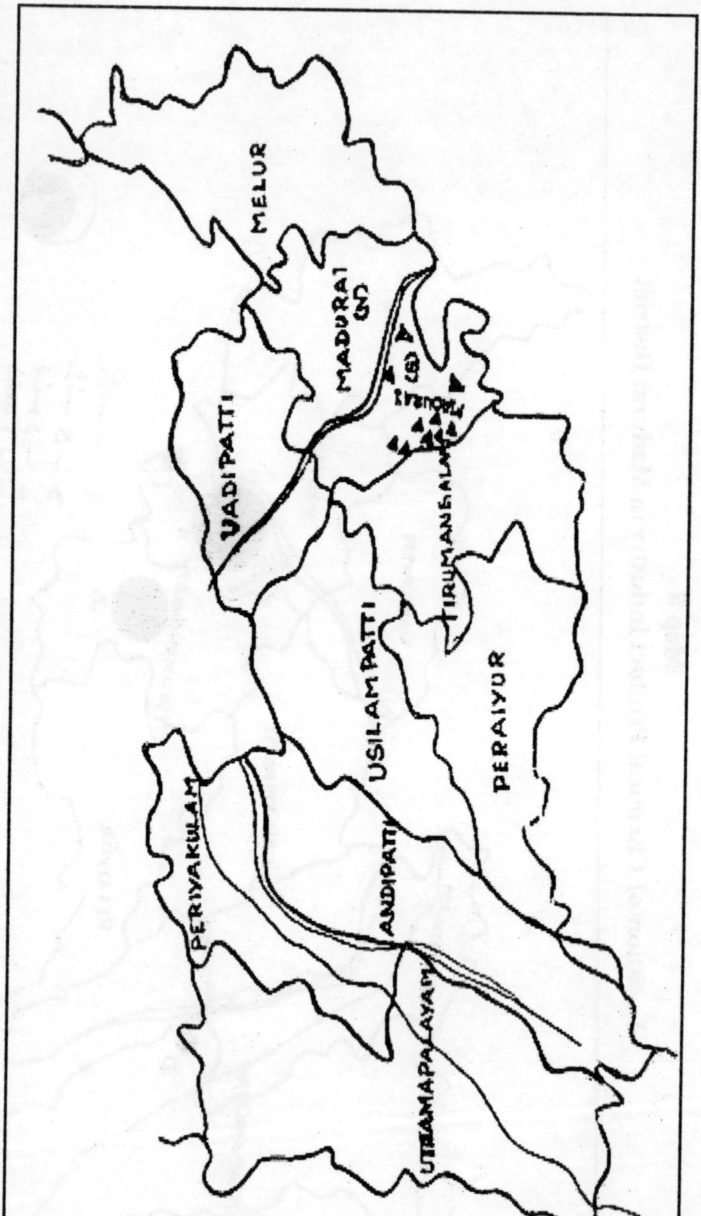

Map 10

Location Density of Electroplating Industry in Madurai District

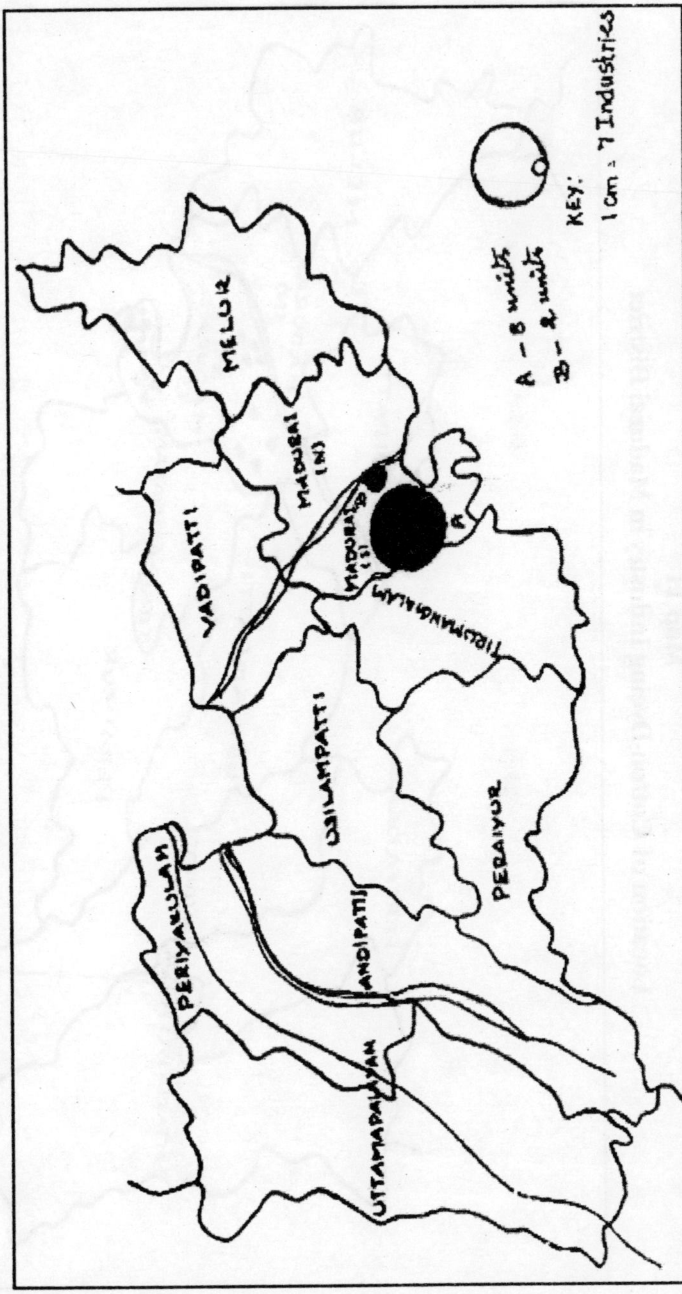

Map 11
Location of Cotton-Dyeing Industry in Madurai District

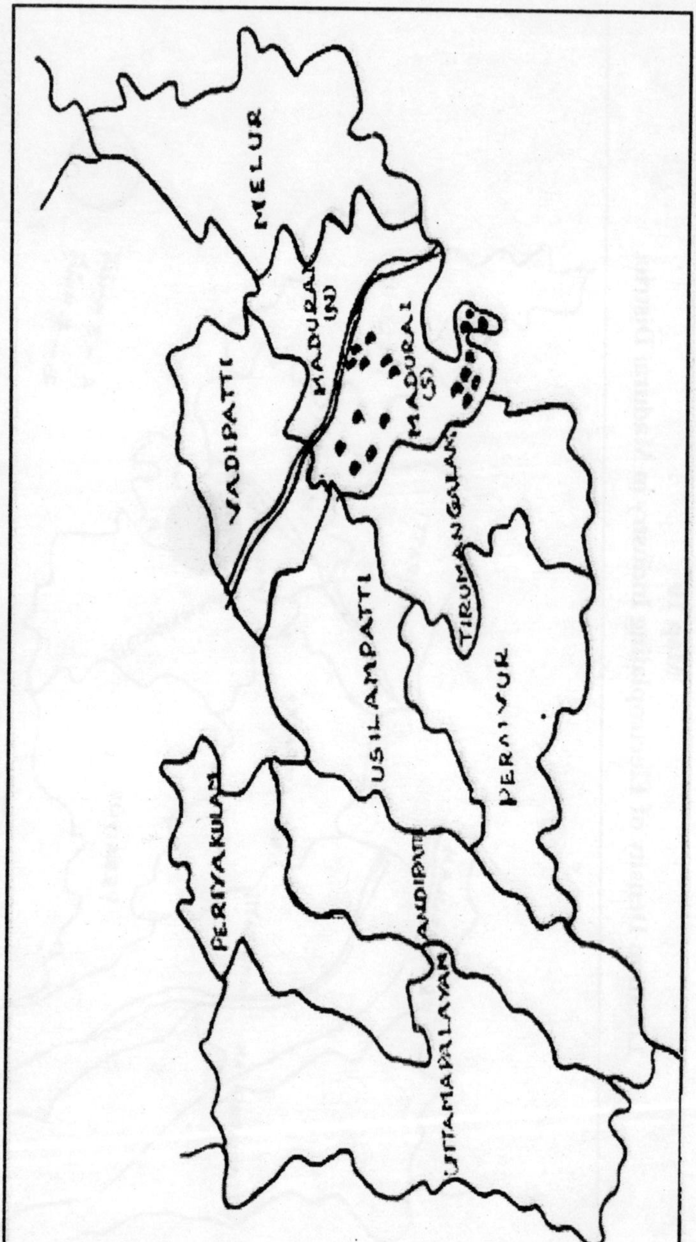

Map 12

Location Density of Cotton-Dyeing Industry in Madurai District

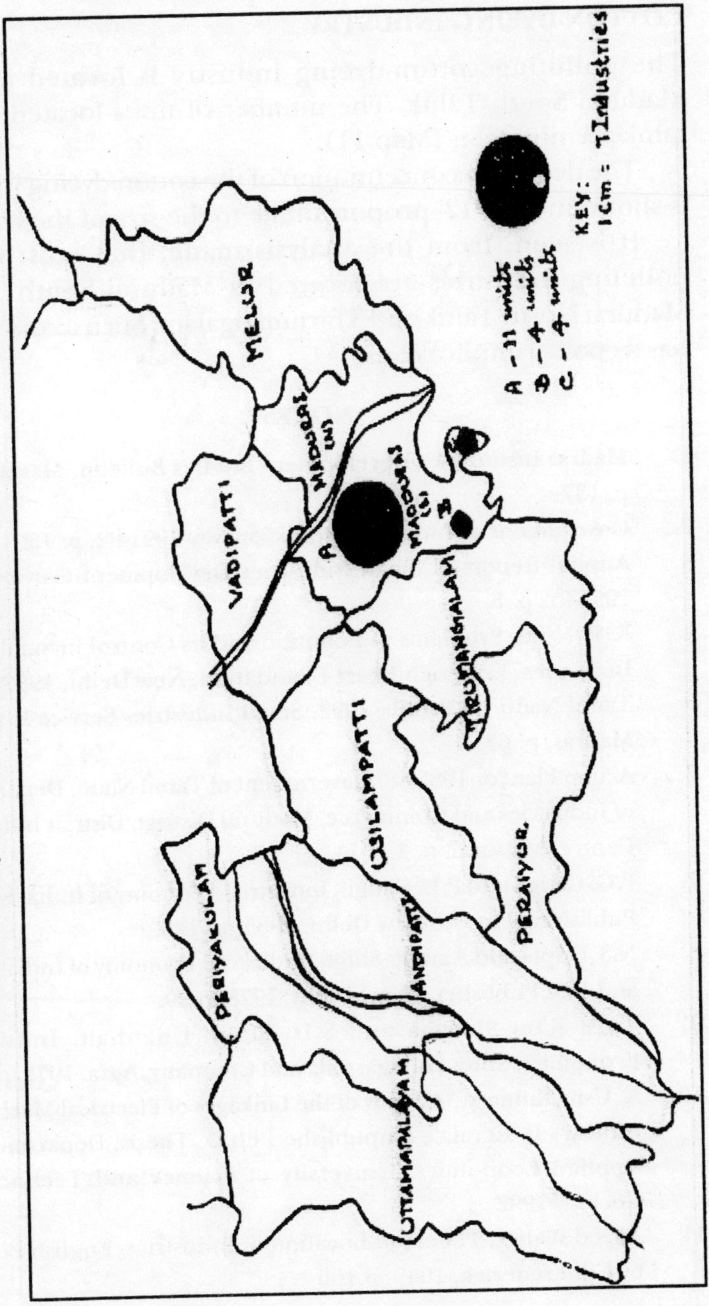

COTTON-DYEING INDUSTRY

The polluting cotton-dyeing industry is located only in Madurai South Taluk. The number of units located in this taluk are nineteen (Map 11).

The degree of concentration of the cotton-dyeing industry is shown in Map 12, proportionate to the size of the circle.

It is seen, from the analysis made, that most of the polluting industries are located in Madurai South Taluk, Madurai North Taluk and Thirumangalam. Such a conclusion has its policy implications.

NOTES

1. Madras Institute of Development Studies Bulletin, March 1993, p. 137.
2. Government of India, Economic Survey 1991-92, p. 15.
3. Annual Report of Small Industries Development Corporation, 1991-92, p. 8.
4. K. P. Nyati, Problems of Pollution and its Control in Small Scale Industries, Friderich Ebert Foundation, New Delhi, 1988, p. 3.
5. Tamil Nadu - A Profile 1992, Small Industries Service Institute, Madras, p. 63.
6. Action Plan for 1985-88, Government of Tamil Nadu, Department of Industries and Commerce, Madurai District, District Industries Centre, Madurai, p. 3.
7. P.G. Gadgil and P.L. Gadgil, Industrial Economy of India, Eurasia Publishing House, New Delhi, 1985, p. 125.
8. N.S. Gupta and Amarjit Singh, Industrial Economy of India, Light and Life Publishers, New Delhi, 1978, p.39.
9. Tulsi Ram Sharma and S.D. Singh Chauhan, Industrial Economics, Shiva Lal Agarwala and Company, Agra, 1972, p. 417.
10. K. Usha Kumary, "A Study of the Linkages of Electrical Machinery Industry in Kerala", Unpublished Ph.D. Thesis, Department of Applied Economics, University of Science and Technology, Cochin, 1992.
11. Alfred Weber, Theory of Location of Industries, English Edition by C.J. Frederick, 1949, p.166.

12. Melvin Greenhut, Plant Location in Theory and Practice, The University of North Carolian Press, 1956, pp. 97-117.
13. P. Sargant Florence, The Logic of British and American Industries, Routedge and Organ Paul Ltd., London, 1972, p. 98.
14. P. G. Gadgil and P. L. Gadgil, Op. Cit., p. 136.
15. N.S. Gupta and Amarjit Singh, Op. Cit., p. 43.
16. Sargant Florence, Investment, Location and Size of Plant, Cambridge, 1948, p. 34.
17. Ch. Uma Maheswara Rao, Small Scale Industries - Some Economic Aspects, Popular Prakashan, Bombay, 1965, pp. 46-47.
18. Ibid., p. 48.
19. Ibid., p. 51.

5

A Profile of Sample Units

INTRODUCTION

The concept of capital-output ratio and labour-output ratio are applicable not only to an economy but also to its different sectors. Productivity represents the composite efforts of all factors contributing to production. As a ratio of productivity relates output to input, it is an indicator of overall efficiency of a firm or industry.

EFFICIENCY

The implications and the means by which efficiency can be measured are not so readily apparent. The difficulty begins with the meaning of the term, 'efficiency'. It can mean an abstract quality, an impression of competence or capability, readily recognised when a person or a piece of an organisation does its work particularly well.

The types of efficiency are Economic efficiency and Technical efficiency.

Economic efficiency implies the avoidance of waste, whether it is waste of human or mechanical effort of productive resources or physical materials. It means the effectiveness in securing the greatest product at a minimum cost to meet a public demand at a remunerative price.[1] It will depend upon personal factors and technical merit. It will also be affected by the organisation and administration of the supervisory function, by the capital cost of plant and equipment in relation to its effective life and output, by the lay out of the factory and by the flow of production through the factory.

To the technologist, 'efficiency' means technical efficiency which in turn can have any of the following meanings. A machine or appliance or organisation is efficient in so far as it is adequate to the demands made on it, or in so far as it lives upto the claims made for it. Efficiency may mean doing a job perfectly in the cheapest possible way.[2]

Thus generally efficiency refers to the relation between return and cost. The three direct tests of efficiency are 1. Productivity, 2. Cost per unit and 3. Return (especially profit).[3]

Productivity is always expressed in physical terms and related to productive efficiency but it does not reflect special purchasing economies or financial arrangements.[4] Productivity is almost invariably taken to mean productivity of labour yet efficiency consists in making the best use of all resources and not just one.

In this study, two productivity ratios are used to measure the productivity of labour and capital. Capital-labour ratio is used to find out whether a particular firm has adopted the capital-intensity technology or labour-intensity technology.

A ratio is simply one number expressed in terms of another number. Any attempt to find out the relationship between two items or groups of items of the financial statement establishes a ratio. Similarly, ratio analysis means the process of computing, determining and presenting the relationship of items and groups of items of the financial statements. Ratio analysis provides inter-firm comparison to measure efficiency and helps the management to take corrective action. "Ratios can assist management in its basic functions of forecasting, planning, co-ordinative control and communication".[5] Ratios have their own limitations in giving reliable conclusions. In spite of certain limitations, "the ratios if discriminatingly calculated and wisely interpreted can be a useful tool of financial analysis".[6]

The capital productivity, labour productivity and capital intensity of 19 sample units of cotton-dyeing industry, 11 units of chemical product industry, 8 units of paint industry, 16 units of soap manufacturing industry and 10 units of electroplating industry are shown in Tables 1, 2, 3, 4 and 5.

Table 1
Cotton-dyeing Industry
(Including the rental value of the building-during 1991-92)

Sl. No.	*Output-Labour Ratio (O/L) (Rs.)*	*Output-Capital Ratio (O/C) (Rs.)*	*Capital-Labour Ratio (C/L) (Rs.)*
1.	51240.00	5.07	10100.00
2.	460600.00	35.71	12900.00
3.	266900.00	29.33	9100.00
4.	427000.00	43.28	9866.67
5.	778720.00	21.60	36050.00
6.	1380526.30	534.76	2581.58
7.	562500.00	112.50	5000.00
8.	366000.00	154.11	2375.00
9.	488000.00	67.00	7283.33
10.	778720.00	18.28	42600.00
11.	164850.00	23.78	6933.33
12.	197820.00	23.44	8440.00
13.	157500.00	28.64	5500.00
14.	224196.00	11.27	19900.00
15.	2185833.30	567.75	3850.00
16.	164850.00	32.32	5100.00
17.	384000.00	41.74	9200.00
18.	1457222.20	993.56	1466.67
19.	369600.00	30.05	12300.00

Source: Survey Data

In Madurai District, there are 369 textile-based units under Small Scale Industries with the total investment of Rs.130.97 lakhs and employment of 3,047 persons contributing an output worth of Rs.2,022.26 lakhs. The overall labour productivity in these textile-based units works out to Rs. 66,368.89.

(a) Output-Labour Ratio

Cotton-dyeing industry is a constitutent in the textile-based industries. In the 19 units which are analysed in the present study, the average labour productivity is relatively high amounting to Rs.8,86,475.74. Among the ninteen units chosen, eighteen units have labour productivity at a higher level than that in the whole of the textile-based industries. This implies that labour contribution is very high in the cotton-dyeing industry when compared to the same in the textile-based industries.

(b) Output-Capital Ratio

In the case of ninteen sample units, the average capital productivity is comparatively high. In fact it is Rs.115.41. The overall capital productivity in the textile-based industries under Small Scale Industries in Madurai District works out to Rs.15.44. Among the ninteen units chosen, seventeen units have capital productivity at a higher level than that in the whole of textile-based industries. This indicates that the capital productivity is very high in the cotton-dyeing industry when compared to the same in the textile-based industries.

(c) Capital-Labour Ratio

In the case of ninteen sample units, the average capital-labour ratio is Rs.7,680.87 which is relatively high. The overall capital intensity in the textile-based factories under Small Scale Industries in Madurai District has been calculated to be Rs.4,298.33. From Table 1 it is obvious that the sixteen sample units of cotton-dyeing industry have the capital intensity at a higher level than that in the whole of the textile-based industries. This denotes that capital intensity technology has been adopted in the cotton-dyeing industry. The capital intensity has increased not only the capital productivity but also the labour productivity of the cotton-dyeing industry.

CHEMICAL PRODUCT INDUSTRY

The output-labour ratio, output-capital and capital-labour ratio of chemical product industry are shown in Table 2.

Table 2

Chemical Product Industry

(Including the Rental Value of the Building-during 1991-92)

Sl. No.	*Output-Labour Ratio (O/L) (Rs.)*	*Output-Capital Ratio (O/C) (Rs.)*	*Capital-Labour Ratio (C/L) (Rs.)*
1.	1098000.00	159.59	6880.00
2.	2243791.70	30.32	74000.00
3.	325333.33	15.06	21600.00
4.	549500.00	4.54	121066.67
5.	2000000.00	13.70	145942.86
6.	132166.67	3.20	41266.67
7.	651000.00	24.57	26500.00
8.	1122400.00	213.79	5250.00
9.	333333.33	9.35	35644.44
10.	587125.00	5.40	108640.00
11.	158600.00	11.47	13822.22

Source: Survey Data.

In Madurai District, there are 709 chemical based units under Small Scale Industries with the total investment of Rs.956.28 lakhs and employment of 6,506 persons, contributing an output worth of Rs.6,269.82 lakhs.

(a) Output-Labour Ratio

In the eleven units which are taken for this study, the average labour productivity is Rs.7,21,742.17 which is relatively high. The overall labour productivity in the chemical-based industries has been calculated at Rs.96,369.81. Chemical product industry is a constitutent in the chemical-based industries. In all the eleven sample units, labour productivity is at a higher level than that in the whole of the chemical-based industries. It indicates that labour productivity is very high in chemical product industry when compared to the same in the chemical-based industries.

(b) Output-Capital Ratio

In the eleven sample units of the chemical product industry, the average capital productivity is Rs.16.91, which is relatively high. The overall capital productivity in the chemical-based industries has been calculated at Rs.6.56. Among the eleven sample units, eight units have capital productivity at a higher level than that in the whole of the chemical-based industries. It implies that capital productivity is very high in the chemical product industry when compared to the same in the chemical-based industries.

(c) Capital-Labour Ratio

In the eleven sample units of chemical product factories, the average capital intensity is Rs.42,691.57 which is relatively high. The overall capital intensity in the chemical-based industries works out to Rs.14,698.43. Among the eleven units chosen, eight units have capital intensity at a higher level than that in the whole of chemical-based industries. This implies that capital intensity is very high in this industry when compared to the same in the chemical-based industries.

PAINT INDUSTRY

The labour productivity, capital productivity and capital intensity of the paint industry are shown in Table 3.

Table 3
Paint Industry
(Including the rental value in Fixed Capital-during 1991-92)

Sl. No.	*Output-Labour Ratio (O/L) (Rs.)*	*Output-Capital Ratio (O/C) (Rs.)*	*Capital-Labour Ratio (C/L) (Rs.)*
1.	1025733.30	58.06	17666.67
2.	1570000.00	95.54	16433.33
3.	250000.00	40.82	6125.00
4.	60000.00	1.68	35800.00
5.	1177500.00	102.39	11500.00
6.	355833.33	8.53	41733.33
7.	1258125.00	65.87	19100.00
8.	711666.67	30.27	23511.11

Source: Survey Data.

(a) Output-Labour Ratio

Paint industry is a constitutent in the chemical-based industries. In the eight units which are analysed in the present study, the average labour productivity is relatively high, amounting to Rs.6,41,243.48. The overall labour productivity in the chemical-based industries has been calculated to be Rs.96,369.81. Among the eight units chosen, seven units have labour productivity at a higher level than that in the whole of the chemical-based industries. This implies that labour contribution is very high in this paint industry when compared to the same in the chemical-based industries.

(b) Output-Capital Ratio

In paint industry, the average capital productivity is Rs.27.42. Among the eight units chosen, seven units have capital productivity at a higher level than that in the whole of the chemical-based industries. The overall capital productivity in the chemical-based industries has been calculated at Rs.6.56. It implies that capital productivity is very high in the paint industry when compared to the same in the chemical-based industries.

(c) Capital-Labour Ratio

The average capital intensity in paint industry is Rs.23,384.78. Among the eight units chosen, six units have capital intensity at a higher level than that in the whole of the chemical-based industries. The overall capital intensity in the chemical-based industries works out to Rs.14,698.43. It shows that the capital intensity is very high in paint industry when compared to the same in the chemical-based industries.

SOAP INDUSTRY

Details of the output-labour ratio, output-capital ratio and capital-labour ratio of the soap industry are presented in Table 4.

Table 4

Soap Industry (Including the rental value of the building in Fixed Capital - during 1991-92)

Sl. No.	*Output-Labour Ratio (O/L) (Rs.)*	*Output-Capital Ratio (O/C) (Rs.)*	*Capital-Labour Ratio (C/L) (Rs.)*
1.	263760.00	54.95	4800.00
2.	100192.50	30.06	3333.33
3.	735000.00	37.00	19866.67
4.	634000.00	20.62	30750.00
5.	1413000.00	33.98	41583.33
6.	1046666.70	37.03	28266.67
7.	1345714.30	39.32	34228.57
8.	630000.00	44.11	14283.33
9.	735000.00	47.42	15500.00
10	262500.00	12.08	21733.33
11	312000.00	13.04	23925.00
12.	27333.00	13.00	21333.33
13.	593947.37	69.83	8505.26
14.	376166.67	43.27	8693.33
15.	630000.00	43.83	14375.00
16.	385000.00	13.70	28111.11

Source: Survey Data.

(a) Output-Labour Ratio

Soap industry is a constitutent in the chemical- based industries. In the sixteen units which are analysed in the present study, the average labour productivity is Rs.6,16,150.35 which is relatively high. The overall labour productivity in the chemical-based industries has been calculated to be Rs. 96,369.81. Among the sixteen units chosen, all the units have labour productivity at a higher level than that in the whole of the chemical-based industries. This shows that average labour contribution is increased by more than six times in soap industry when compared to the same in the chemical-based industries.

(b) Output-Capital Ratio

In the soap industry, the average capital productivity is Rs.30.67. The overall capital productivity in the chemical-based industries is Rs.6.56. Among the sixteen units chosen, all the units have capital productivity at a higher level than that in the whole of the chemical-based industries. This implies that the capital contribution is very high in the soap industry when compared to the same in the chemical-based industries.

(c) Capital-Labour Ratio

The average capital intensity in soap industry is Rs. 20,087.96. The overall capital intensity in the chemical-based industries works out to Rs.14,698.43. Among the sixteen units chosen, ten units have capital intensity at a higher level than that in the whole of the chemical-based industries. It denotes that capital intensity is high in soap industry when compared to the same in the chemical-based industries.

ELECTROPLATING INDUSTRY

Details of the labour productivity, capital productivity and capital intensity of electroplating industry are given in Table 5.

Table 5

Electroplating Industry

(Including the rental value of the building - during 1991-92)

Sl. No.	Output-Labour Ratio (O/L) (Rs.)	Output-Capital Ratio (O/C) (Rs.)	Capital-Labour Ratio (C/L) (Rs.)
1.	75360.00	5.53	13632.00
2.	1176791.70	26.92	43716.67
3.	25498.00	1.34	19066.67
4.	941433.33	26.05	36133.33
5.	62800.00	5.62	11166.67
6.	7575.00	0.84	8950.00
7.	55200.00	2.92	18880.00
8.	81326.00	1.94	42040.00
9.	6285.71	4.13	11200.00
10.	25498.00	0.98	26000.00

Source: Survey Data.

(a) Output-Labour Ratio

In Madurai District, there are 1,536 engineering- based units under Small Scale Industries with the total investment of Rs.774.91 lakhs and employment of 8,438 persons contributing an output worth of Rs.10,477.68 lakhs.

Electroplating industry is a constitutent in the engineering-based industries. In the ten units taken for this study, the average labour productivity is Rs.4,01,516.21 which is relatively high. The overall labour productivity in the engineering-based industries has been calculated at Rs.1,24,172.55. Among the ten units chosen, only two units have labour productivity at a higher level than that in the whole of the engineering-based industries. It indicates that labour productivity is very low in electroplating industry when compared to the same in the engineering-based industries.

(b) Output-Capital Ratio

In electroplating industry, the average capital productivity is Rs.15.12 which is relatively high. Among the ten units chosen, only two units have capital productivity at a higher level than that in the whole of the engineering-based industries. The overall capital productivity in the engineering-based units works out to Rs.13.52. It implies that the capital productivity is very low in electroplating industry when compared to the same in the engineering-based industries.

(c) Capital-Labour Ratio

The average capital intensity in electroplating industry is Rs. 26,550.13 which is three times higher than that of the capital intensity of engineering-based industries. The overall capital intensity in the engineering-based industries works out to Rs.9,183.57. Among the ten units chosen, nine units have capital intensity at a higher level than that in the whole of the engineering-based industries. This implies that the capital intensity is very high in the electroplating industry when compared to the same in the engineering- based industries.

It is necessary to assess the average productivity of capital and labour. In order to find out the performance of sample units, average output-labour ratio, output-capital ratio and capital-labour ratio of the five categories are calculated.

The average output-labour ratio, output-capital ratio and capital-labour ratio of the five categories of Small Scale Industries are given in Table 6.

Average labour productivity is higher in the cotton-dyeing industry. It is lower in the electroplating industry. Average capital productivity is higher in cotton-dyeing industry. It is lower in electroplating industry. Average capital intensity is higher in chemical product industry. It is lower in the cotton-dyeing industry.

Data collected from Small Scale Industries fall under the two digit NIC Codes, which are brought out by the Statistics and Data Bank Division, Ministry of Industry, Government of India, New Delhi.

Table 6

Overall Small Scale Industries Ratio

(Including the rental value of the building-during 1991-92)

Sl. No.	*Type of the Industry*	*Output-Labour Ratio (O/L) (Rs.)*	*Output-Capital Ratio (O/C) (Rs.)*	*Capital-Labour Ratio (C/L) (Rs.)*
1.	Soap Industry	616150.35	30.67	20087.96
2.	Paint Industry	641243.48	27.42	23384.78
3.	Chemical Product Industry	721742.17	16.91	42691.57
4.	Cotton-Dyeing Industry	886475.74	115.41	7680.87
5.	Electroplating Industry	401516.21	15.12	26550.13

Source: Survey Data.

To compare the sample units with the Madurai District as a whole, sample units of the five categories are to be grouped under the three categories of NIC Codes such as textile-based industries, chemical-based industries and engineering-based Industries.

TEXTILE-BASED INDUSTRIES

Textile-based industries include cotton ginning and baling, cotton cleaning, spinning and weaving of cotton textiles, dyeing and bleaching of cotton textiles, dyeing of cloth and yarn, printing of cloth and production of khadi.

The particulars about the textile-based industries and the details of the labour productivity, capital productivity and capital intensity of these industries are given in Tables 7 and 8 respectively.

CHEMICAL-BASED INDUSTRIES

The chemical-based industries consist of manufacture of heavy inorganic chemicals, basic heavy organic chemicals, pesticides, paints, varnishes, dyestuffs, drugs and medicines, washing soap and its powder and textile chemical auxiliaries.

Table 7
Textile-based Industries - Details

Sl. No.	*Particulars*	*During 1991-92*
1.	Number of units (SSI)	369.00
2.	Investment (Rs. in lakhs)	130.97
3.	Output (Rs. in lakhs)	2022.26
4.	Labour (in numbers)	3047.00

Source: District Industries Centre, Madurai.

Table 8
Textile-based Industries - Ratios

Sl. No.	*Ratios*	*During 1991-92*
1.	Output-Labour Ratio (O/L)	66368.89
2.	Output-Capital Ratio (O/C)	15.44
3.	Capital-Labour Ratio (C/L)	4298.33

Source: Computed Data.

Details of the chemical-based industries are presented in Table 9 and the ratios of the chemical-based industries are given in Table 10.

Table 9
Chemical-based Industries – Details

Sl. No.	*Particulars*	*During 1991-92*
1.	Number of units (SSI)	709.00
2.	Investment (Rs. in lakhs)	956.28
3.	Output (Rs. in lakhs)	6269.82
4.	Labour (in numbers)	65.06.00

Source: District Industries Centre, Madurai.

Table 10
Chemical based Industries - Ratios

Sl. No.	*Ratios*	*During 1991-92*
1.	Output-Labour Ratio (O/L)	93369.81
2.	Output-Capital Ratio (O/C)	6.56
3.	Capital-Labour Ratio (C/L)	14698.43

Source: Computed Data.

ENGINEERING-BASED INDUSTRIES

Engineering-based industries cover manufacture of iron and steel, manufacture of castings and forgings, non-ferrous sheet, melting and refining of aluminium metal, zinc products, manufacture of safes, vaults and almirahs, manufacture of bolts and nuts, locks, metal chains, electroplating, kitchen gadgets and manufacture of parts and accessories and general hardwares.

Details of the engineering-based industries are given in Table 11 and the ratios of the engineering-based industries are given in Table 12.

Table 11
Engineering-based Industries - Details

Sl. No.	*Particulars*	*During 1991-92*
1.	Number of units (SSI)	1536.00
2.	Investment (Rs. in lakhs)	774.91
3.	Output (Rs. in lakhs)	10477.68
4.	Labour (in numbers)	8438.00

Source: District Industries Centre, Madurai.

Table 12
Engineering-based Industries - Ratios

Sl. No.	*Ratios*	*During 1991-92*
1.	Output-Labour Ratio (O/L)	124172.55
2.	Output-Capital Ratio (O/C)	13.52
3.	Capital-Labour Ratio (C/L)	9183.57

Source: Computed Data.

The analysis undertaken shows that the average level of capital productivity and labour productivity are high in chemical product, cotton-dyeing, paint and soap industries, while they are low in electroplating industry. The average capital intensity is low in cotton-dyeing units among the five categories of sample units. The low capital productivity in electroplating units is mainly due to the lack of willingness to go in for new sophisticated techniques.

The above analysis indicates the status of factor productivities in polluting Small Scale Industries. Productivity and modernisation are complementary to each other. Unless modernisation is done, productivity cannot be improved. The labour productivity can be increased by offering proper training to workers. The Small Scale Industries do not have adequate finance. As they have limited capital resources they find it difficult to introduce modern technology which alone can increase the growth rate. The use of highly capital-intensive techniques can lead to the production of quality products and lowering costs and more profits. The Small Scale Industrial Sector should be assured of financial adequacy to enable it to introduce modern technology and innovative techniques. These measures may help to improve the efficiency of these industries on the one hand and minimise the negative effects on the other, which cause environmental damage.

NOTES

1. L.C. Hawkins, "Measurement of Efficiency", Oxford Economic Papers, New Series, Vol. 11, No. 1, 1950, pp. 30-31.
2. H. Speight, Economics and Industrial Efficiency, An Introduction to Managerial Economics, Macmillan, Third Edition, New Delhi, 1970, pp. 1-2.
3. P. Sargant Florence, The Logic of British and American Industry, London, 1961, p. 53.
4. W. Kendrick John and Geamer Daniel, Measuring Company Productivity, New York, 1961, p. 7.

5. J. Batty, Management Accounting, Macdonald and Evans Ltd., London, 1970, p. 413.
6. Hunt Williams and Donaldson, Basic Business Finance, Richard D. Irwin Inc., Home Wood Illinois, 1971, pp. 116-126.

6

A Profile of Sample Units

Water pollution, caused by two types of industries namely electroplating and cotton-dyeing is analysed in the present chapter. The other sample industry, namely chemical-based, in which soap, paint and chemical product units are studied, does not produce water pollution problem, as some of the units do not use water as raw material while others use water as raw material, but from which effluents are not produced.

Water is one of the most important requirements for life. It is available through various rivers, streams and wells in the country. But the rivers and the streams are also used for letting out industrial wastes from the industries situated near about. Industrial wastes contain mineral and organic substances, acids, alkalies, salts, oils, grease and variety of poisonous substances including radioactive materials which are highly toxic to human, animal and plant life. When a stream receives such untreated wastes from an industry it adds to the pollution load of water, causing deterioration in physical, chemical, biological and bacteriological quality of water.

INDUSTRY AND ENVIRONMENT

There is an increasing tendency in the environmental pollution. water is polluted by two kinds of wastes; traditional organic waste and waste generated by industrial processes. While it is estimated that municipal sources generate three fourths of the waste water, industrial waste, though small in volume, contributes over one third of the total pollutant load, and half of this is contributed by large and medium industries.[1]

It is significant that industries that consume more energy, water, wood and other resources usually generate more residuals and pollutants. With rapid industrialisation, industrial wastes have also been growing in volume. The subject of industry and environment is a complex one and it is difficult to identify or find any easy solution.

A survey of industrial cities of India has shown that industrial waste water constitutes by volume between 8 to 16 per cent of the total waste water generated - the remaining 84 to 92 per cent being generated from the domestic sector. With rapid industrialisation, the waste water from the industrial sector is expected to rise to 33 per cent by A.D. 2000.[2]

Wastes from industries vary with the nature of the plant, the designs and the raw materials used. The industrial effluents include raw materials, processed chemicals, final products, process intermediates, other by-products and impurities as pollutants.[3] Industries contribute to air, water and land pollution. The major types of industries in India that contribute significantly to pollution problems are the tanneries, the textiles, sugar factories, distillaries, dairies, fertilizers, oil refineries and steel mills.

Today Industry is responsible for more than twice as much pollution as is the domestic sewage in the western world. Some industrial effluents are actually more serious than household waste, for besides containing organic material, they may include inorganic compounds like salfuric acid, arsenic and cyanides, which are difficult to remove and highly poisonous.[4] Suspended solids settle out particularly in lakes and reservoirs. If too much waste is present, oxygen is removed from the water, faster than it can be replenished. Decomposition is then taken over by anaerobic bacteria, which produce obnoxious or toxic compounds such as methane and hydrogen sulphide. The water is then both a public nuisance and unfit for use.

The present study takes into account two types of small scale units namely cotton-dyeing and electroplating which cause water pollution.

COTTON-DYEING UNITS

Dyeing is carried out with varied types of dyes. The quality and to a certain extent, the quantity of the effluent depend on the type of dyeing. The Researcher has examined three types of dyes, namely direct dyes, vat dyes and naphthol dyes.

DIRECT DYES

In most of the small dyeing units direct dyes are used as they are easy to apply and no auxiliary chemicals such as mordants are needed. In this dyeing process, soap oil, soda ash, dyeing colours and bleaching liquid are used as raw materials. The cost of direct dyeing is low compared to others. Though the colour is stable for washing, their colour fastness is not so appreciable.

VAT DYES

These are water insoluble and fast dyes applied along with strong reducing agents (sodium hydro-sulphide) and alkali to make the dye soluble. Vat green FFB, caustic soda, hydro sulphate, bleaching liquor and non-edible oil are used as raw materials in the vat dyeing process. Hot water is used to prepare chemical solution. The cloth is exposed to air for oxidation. The excess alkali remaining on the cloth is neutralised by scouring, that is, treatment with dilute solution of acid. The colour is more stable for washing. The cost of dyeing is very high.

NAPHTHOL DYES

Betanaphthol is first applied to the fabric, dried and then treated with a developer for coupling and diazotisation after which the color is formed. This is followed by soaping and alkali treatment. Naphthol AS, caustic soda, soda ash, sodium nitrate, acitated hydrochloric acid, soap oil and alumina are used as raw materials in this process. Cool water is used to prepare chemical solution. The colour is slightly unstable for washing. This type of dyeing generates more volume of effluents, compared to the other two.

ELECTROPLATING UNITS

In electroplating industry, as the name implies, base metals are plated for protection from corrosion, for brightness and for fair appearance.The platings usually are chromium, nickel, zinc, cadmium, copper, silver and gold. The plating operations are preceded by cleaning and stripping which generate strong effluents in significant quantities.

The present study concentrates on nickel plating. In nickel plating units, nickel solution is prepared. It contains nickel sulphate, nickel chloride, boric acid and caustic soda. Nickel solution, chromium salt and nickel anode are used as raw materials for plating the metals.

In both cotton-dyeing and electroplating industries, the water pollution parameters, Biochemical Oxygen Demand (BOD) and Chemical Oxygen Demand (COD) are measured with the help of waste water released from the concerned industry. The waste effluent depends upon the volume of output produced by the industry which in turn determines the quantity of waste water.

A regression analysis helps to predict the unknown values of one variable from known values of another variable. With the help of the waste water released from cotton-dyeing and electroplating industries, water pollution parameters namely BOD and COD are estimated. It reveals the average relationship between the above two variables.

The simple regression model is used to assess the impact of the quantity of waste water released on water pollution parameters namely BOD and COD. The model estimated is

Y = a + b X

X stands for quantity of waste water in litres and

Y refers to the water pollution parameters in kilograms.

Therefore, Y = BOD and COD).

The simple regression model for cotton-dyeing units is explained in Table 1.

Table 1

Simple Regression Model For Cotton-dyeing Industry

Y = a + b X

Sl. No.	*Name of the water pollution parameters*	*a*	*b*	R^2	*F*
1.	BOD	-16670.61	120.59*	0.9052	162.36
			(19248.62)	(9.464)	
2.	COD	-52263.619	599.64*	0.9139	180.52
			(90772.272)	(44.63)	

Source: Survey Data

Note: * Significant at 1 per cent level.

Figures in brackets refer to the Standard Error.

BOD - Biochemical Oxygen demand

COD - Chemical Oxygen demand

The influence of quantity of waste water on water pollution load is highly significant at 1 per cent level. In cotton-dyeing industry the co-efficient of determination in the case of BOD is 0.9052 which implies that 90 per cent of variation in dependent variable is, that is, water pollution load BOD has been explained by the independent variable, that is, quantity of waste water.

In the case of COD, R^2 is equal to 0.9139 which denotes that the model is able to explain 91 per cent variation of the dependent variable, that is, COD. This model explains a satisfactory level of variation in 'Y' that is, in water pollution parameters.

In fact, an increase of one kilolitre of waste water would result in water pollution load of 120.590 kg in BOD and 599.640 kg in COD.

Comparing the influence of waste water and water pollution load (BOD and COD) in the cotton-dyeing industry, it is observed that COD is greater than BOD.

The simple regression model for elctroplating units is estimated and given in Table 2.

Table 2

Simple Regression Model For Electorplating Industry

Y = a + b X

Sl. No.	*Name of the water pollution parameters*	*a*	*b*	R^2	*F*
1.	BOD	0.0013	0.0029*	1.0	2180000000
		(0.0011)	(0. 000000006)		
2.	COD	0.005	0.0021*	1.0	63300000000
		(0.0014)	(0.0000000083)		

Source: Survey Data.

Note: * Significant at 1 per cent level.

Figures in brackets refer to the Standard Error.

The influence of quantity of waste water on water pollution load is highly significant at 1 per cent level in the electroplating industry. In the electroplating industry, the co-efficient of determination for BOD and COD is 1 which would mean that 100 per cent of variation in the dependent variable (BOD and COD) is explained by the model. This model explains a satisfactory level of variation in 'Y' that is, water pollution parameters.

In fact an increase in one kilolitre of waste water would lead to produce water pollution load of 0.29 kg. in BOD and 2.1 kg in COD.

Comparing the influence of waste water on water pollution load (BOD and COD) in electroplating industry, it is observed that COD is heavier than BOD. In both the industries COD is heavier than BOD. Comparing the influence of waste water and water pollution load in both the industries, COD is higher in the cotton-dyeing industry than in the electroplating industry.

IMPLICATION

Natural substances both inorganic and organic present in the effluent, exert an immediate oxygen demand. The stream will then be devoid of oxygen and the aquatic life will be affected adversely.[5]

ANOVA Model - Variation in Water Pollution load in three types of Cotton-Dyeing Industry

There are three types of Cotton-dyeing processes.

1. Naphthol dyes,
2. Vat dyes and
3. Direct dyes.

An analysis of variance is attempted in order to examine whether water pollution load varies in the three types or not. Table 3 shows the total level and the average level of BOD in the three types of cotton-dyeing industry.

Table 3

Average Level of BOD In The Three Types of Cotton-Dyeing Industry (1991-92)

Sl. No.	*Name of the three types*	*Water total (in littres)*	*Average level of water (in littres)*	*BOD total for all units (in grams)*	*BOD average per unit (in grams)*
1.	Naphthol dyes	14702800.00	3675700.00	1823147.20	455786.80
2.	Vat dyes	1502795.00	250465.83	447832.91	74638.82
3.	Direct dyes	6175058.00	686117.55	111151.04	12350.12

Source: Survey Data.

Table 4 explains both the total and the average level of COD in the three types of cotton-dyeing industry.

Table 4

Average Level of Cod in the Three Types of Cotton-dyeing Industry (1991-92)

Sl.	*Name of the three types*	*Total for all units (in grams)*	*Average per unit (in grams)*
1.	Naphthol dyes	9115736.00	2278934.00
2.	Vat dyes	2404472.00	400745.33
3.	Direct dyes	803931.55	89325.73

Source: Survey Data.

It is observed from Tables 3 and 4 that the average level of BOD and COD is higher in naphthol dyes, compared to the other two types.

Simple bar diagrams are used to know this easily. The results have also been shown in the accompanying Figure 1.

Figure 1

Average Level of BOD and COD in Cotton-Dyeing

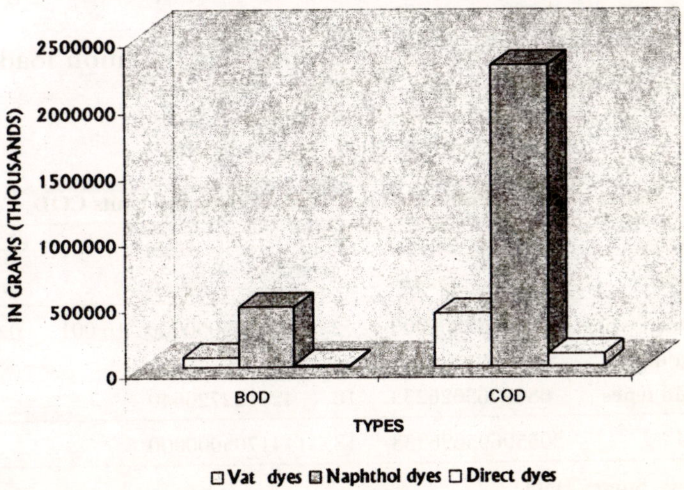

The one way anova of water pollution load presents the following results. Table 5 denotes the anova of water pollution load in cotton-dyeing units, namely BOD.

Table 5

Anova of Water Pollution Load in Cotton-Dyeing Units - BOD

Sources of variation	*Sum of Squares*	*DF*	*Mean Square*	*F*	*Significant F*
Between types of dyeing	567104410725	2	283552205362	16.679	0.000
Within types	272009482887	16	17000592680		
Total	839113893611	18	46617438534		

Source: Survey Data.

The result shows that there is significant difference in water pollution load - BOD among the three types of cotton-dyeing units. Taking into consideration the average value of BOD and COD, Naphthol dyes has the highest water pollution load. Vat dyes has lesser average value of BOD and the direct dyes has the lowest average level of BOD. More chemicals are used in naphthol dyes process which lead to produce higher level of water effluents.

Table 6 illustrates the anova of water pollution load in cotton-dyeing units, namely COD.

Table 6

Anova of Water Pollution Load In Cotton-dyeing Units-COD

Sources of variation	*Sum of Squares*	*DF*	*Mean Square*	*F*	*Significant F*
Between types of dyeing	13700732000000	2	6850366000000	16.001	0.000
Within types	6849963626233	16	428122726640		
Total	20550695626233	18	1141705000000		

Source: Survey Data.

It is observed from Table 6.5 that the BOD level may vary depending upon the volume of waste water let out from the unit. Therefore the BOD levels are worked out for 1000 litres of waste water in the units and then the anova model is attempted.

Table 7 and 9 explain the ANOVA of water pollution load in cotton-dyeing units for 1000 litres of waste water, namely BOD and COD respectively.

Table 7

Anova of Water Pollution Load In Cotton-dyeing Units For 1000 Litres of Waste Water-BOD

Sources of variation	*Sum of Squares*	*DF*	*Mean Square*	*F*	*Significant F*
Between types of dyeing	4914785.007	2	2457392.503	38.077	0.000
Within types	1032589.441	16	64536.840		
Total	5947374.447	18	330409.692		

Source: Survey Data.

Table 8 presents both the total and average level of BOD in the three types of cotton-dyeing units.

Table 8

The Total and Average Level of Bod For 1000 Litres of Waste Water

Sl. No.	*Name of the three types*	*Total for all units (in grams)*	*Average per unit (in grams)*
1.	Naphthol dyes	1788	298
2.	Vat dyes	496	124
3.	Direct dyes	162	18

Source: Survey Data.

There is significant difference between the three types of cotton-dyeing units in producing water effluent, BOD. The average level of BOD in direct dyes is 18 grams, in vat dyes 124 grams and in naphthol dyes 298 grams.

Table 9

Anova of Water Pollution Load In Cotton-dyeing Units For 1000 Litres of Waste Water - COD

Sources of variation	*Sum of Squares*	*DF*	*Mean Square*	*F*	*Significant F*
Between types of dyeing	129323005.134	2	64661502.567	29.786	0.000
Within types	34734296.545	16	2170893.534		
Total	164057301.679	18	9114294.538		

Source: Survey Data.

The result shows that there is significant difference between the three types of cotton-dyeing units.

Table 10 presents both the total and average level of COD in the three types of cotton-dyeing units.

After COD levels are worked out for 1000 litres of waste water in the units, the average level of COD in direct dyes is 144 grams, in vat dyes 620 grams and in naphthol dyes 1600 grams.

Table 10

The Total And Average Level of COD For 1000 Litres of Waste Water

Sl. No.	*Name of the three types*	*Total for all units (in grams)*	*Average per unit (in grams)*
1.	Naphthol dyes	9600	1600
2.	Vat dyes	2480	620
3.	Direct dyes	1296	144

Source: Survey Data.

TESTING OF HYPOTHESIS

The hypothesis underlying the present analysis is that the cotton-dyeing is a major water polluting industry in Madurai.

While analysing the water pollution in two industries, namely cotton-dyeing and electroplating, comparing the influence of waste water and water pollution load in both the industries, it is higher in the cotton-dyeing industry than in the electroplating industry. In fact, an increase in one kilolitre of waste water would lead to produce water pollution load of 120.590 kg. in BOD, and 599.640 kg. in COD, in the cotton-dyeing industry, and 0.29 kg in BOD and 2.1 kg. in COD in the electroplating industry.

Thus cotton-dyeing industry which forms a part of the textile-based industries, is a water polluting industry. While emphasising its economic role, the government has to concentrate on its environmental implications.

Having realised the growing menace of the problem, the Government of India enacted the Water (Prevention and Control of Pollution) Act, 1974 and formed the Central Board for Prevention and Control of Water Pollution. It is necessary that strict action is taken against the polluter. The Government agencies should check and confirm whether the industries adhere strictly to the norms prescribed. Besides more towns should be provided with adequate sewerage facilities and sewage treatment plants. Only these measures can save water from being polluted further.

NOTES

1. "Draft Policy Statement on Pollution Control in India", World Focus, Vol. 12, No. 1, January 1991, p. 19.
2. T.N. Tiwari and Manzoor Ali, Water Quality Index For Indian Rivers, Rourkela, 1982, p. 274.
3. B.K. Senapati, "Man, Technology and Environment-III (In Relati on to Soil)", Ed. by Bhabagrahi Misra, Man, Technology and Environment, Asian Workers' Development Institute, Rourkela, 1987, p. 73.

4. Arun C. Vakil, Economic Aspects of Environmental Pollution in India, Published by Arun C. Vakil, Bombay, 1984, pp. 29-30.
5. N. Manivasakam, Industrial Effluents -Origin, Characteristics, Effects, Analysis and Treatment, Sakthi Publications, Coimbatore, 1987, p. 71.

7

Air Pollution- An Analysis

Air pollution, caused by two types of industries namely cotton-dyeing and soap manufacturing, is analysed in the present chapter. The other sample units, paint and chemical industries do not create any air pollution problem. Because most of the units use electricity as their energy source. But in the cotton-dyeing industry firewood and kerosene are used as energy sources. In the case of soap manfacturing units, firewood is used. The cotton-dyeing and soap industries produce emissions like particulates, sulphur dioxide, oxides of nitrogen, hydrocarbons and carbon monoxide.

INTRODUCTION

The air is one of the most used and abused components of the biosphere. The life support system on this planet consists of air, water, land, flora and fauna. Normally these are mutually interconnected and also inter- dependent. The activities of man constitute one single factor which often disrupts the intricate balance among the foregoing constituents of the life-support system.[1]

Air covers every part of the two hundred million square miles of earth's surface. An average human breathes 22000 times each day taking in approximately 20000 C.C. of air and along with it, 1600 million dust particles.[2]

DEFINITION

Air pollution is the presence of foreign matter in the air which is deterimental to the health and welfare of man. This definition enables us to include not only the direct effects of air pollution on man, but the effects of air pollution which damages materials and reduces the aesthetic value of animate and inanimate matter.[3]

SOURCES OF AIR POLLUTION

On the basis of nature and effects, sources of air pollution may be classified as under

Domestic Sources

Air pollution may arise due to the basic needs of individuals which include domestic fire and domestic incineration which are required for cooking and heating. It is a weak and inevitable source of air pollution. In developing countries, firewood is the main energy source for the vast rural population.

Mobile Vehicles

Mobile Vehicles include road vehicles, air crafts, ships, railways and other vehicles with combustion engines. With a constant increase in the number of vehicles of old types, the problem of air pollution, particularly in towns and cities with a hot climate, is assuming great importance. Though the number of motor vehicles in Indian cities is far less than in cities in the West, the pollution level is almost the same. This is mainly due to the lack of maintenance of Indian vehicles and the absence of any effective deterrent to plying such vehicles on city roads.[4]

Industry

Industry is the principal source of air pollution and it covers all types of units which consume energy in any form, which includes coal, oil, natural gas, electricity and nuclear fission.

Dark smoke emitted by industries pollute the air on a large scale. Industry has a right to produce and make profit, but it has no right to ruin the environment.[5]

Air Pollution in India

Air pollution in India is basically due to the emission of smoke, sulphur dioxide, carbon monoxide and dust fall. The degree of air pollution depends upon some relevant factors like population density, industrial development, geographical situation and the social and economic structures.

Delhi, Bombay and Calcutta suffer largely from air pollution due to excessive concentration of big factories in very small areas and the overload of traffic on a few key routes, resulting in the pollution of the atmosphere. While in the world 300 million tonnes of pollutants are emitted annually in the air, India contributes about 10 million tonnes in the form of particulates, sulphur dioxide, carbon monoxide and hydro carbons.[6] Air pollution in India occurs in isolated pockets because industrial production is concentrated in eight to ten large cities.

The present study concentrates on two industries namely cotton-dyeing and soap manufacturing, which cause air pollution. In both industries, air pollution load under each category is assessed. The consumption level of firewood depends upon the amount of output produced by the factories.

In the soap manufacturing units, two types of washing soaps, namely oil soap and detergent soap, are produced. Firewood is not used in the detergent soap manufacturing unit. But in the oil soap producing unit, firewood is used to heat the water which is mixed with raw materials such as non-edible oil, caustic soda and sodium silicate.

In most of the units of the soap industry and cotton-dyeing industry, the major fuel is firewood. The burning of firewood results in air pollution in terms of particulate matter, Sulphur dioxide (So2), oxides of nitrogen (Nox), Hydrocarbons (HC) and carbon monoxide (Co). The level of air pollution depends upon the quantity of output produced. Therefore, an attempt is made to examine the influence of output on the air pollution load under different categories. Simple Regresion Model is used.

The model is estimated

$$Y = a + b X$$

Where,

X- refers to the output of cotton-dyeing industries in kilograms and

Y- stands for air pollution load under each category in kilograms.

Therefore, Y denotes particulate matter, sulphur dioxide, oxides of nitrogen, hydrocarbons and carbon monoxide which are calculated on the basis of the quantum of firewood used.

The present study takes into account 14 cotton- dyeing units and 10 soap manufacturing units. In the 14 cotton-dyeing units 73,16,807 kg. of firewood are required for the production of 84,01,619 kg. In the 10 soap manufacturing units 4,05,600 kg. of firewood are required for the production of 42,13,000 kg. The results of the estimated models for the five categories in cotton-dyeing units and soap units are given in Tables 1 and 2 respectively.

The influence of quantity of output on the air pollution load under different categories is significant at 1 per cent level.

In Air pollution load under different categories namely particulates, Sulphur dioxide, Oxides of nitrogen, Hydrocarbons and Carbon Monoxide, the co-efficient of determination is 57 per cent which means that 57 per cent of the variation, that is, air pollution load is explained by the independent variable, that is, output in cotton- dyeing industry.

An increase of output by one tonne would result in air pollution loads under different categories, of 11.1 kg, 6.3 kg, 2.2 kg, 0.1 kg, and 0.6 kg, of particulates, sulphur dioxide, oxides of nitrogen, hydro carbons and carbon monoxide respectively in cotton-dyeing industry.

Table 1
Simple Regression Model For Cotton-dyeing Industry
Y = A + B X

Sl. No.	*Name of the Air Pollution Load*	*a*	*b*	R^2	*F*
1.	Particulates	2440.38	0.0111*	0.5795	16.54
		(2531.64)	(0.0027)		
2.	Sulphur Dioxide (So_2)	3580.41	0.0163*	0.5795	16.54
		(3714.31)	(0.0040)		
3.	Oxides of Nitrogen (NO_x)	484.51	0.0022*	0.5795	16.54
		(502.63)	(0.0005)		
4.	Hydrocarbons (HC)	24.94	0.0001*	0.5795	16.54
		(25.87)	(0.000027)		
5.	Carbon Monoxide (Co)	133.55	0.0006*	0.5795	16.54
		(138.60)	(0.00014)		

Source: Survey Data.

Note: * Significant at 1 per cent level.
(Figures in brackets refer to the Standard Error)

Comparing the influence of output and air pollution load under different categories in cotton-dyeing industry it is observed that particulates are greater than sulphur dioxide which in turn, is greater than oxides of nitrogen. The other two namely hydrocarbons and carbon monoxide are present in very small quantities.

IMPLICATIONS

Particulates

The effects of particulates on plants are less harmful. They cause an increase in the fluoride content of the leaves and occasional tip-burn. But the growth and yield are not much affected. The ingestion by the cattle of various fluorine compounds for ages, causes abnormal calcification of bones and teeth called flurosis, eventually resulting in loss of weight.[7]

Particulate pollutants enter the human body almost exclusively through the respiratory system. Hence they affect this system almost immediately. The intensity of the effects depend on the degree of particulate penetration within the system, and the particulate toxicity.[8]

SULPHUR DIOXIDE

Sulphur dioxide causes suffocation as well as throat and eye irritation. It also creates some respiratory diseases both in animals and human beings. In the case of vegetation, sulphur dioxide causes foliar interveinous chlorosis and necrosis.[9]

Simple regression model for soap manufacturing units is estimated and given in Table 2. 'X 'stands for output of soap manufacturing units in kilograms and 'Y' stands for air pollution load under each category in kilograms. The regression model for 10 units is estimated.

Table 7.2

Simple Regression Model For Soap Industry

Y = A + B X

Sl. No.	*Name of the Air Pollution Load*	*a*	*b*	R^2	*F*
1.	Particulates	113.71**	0.0010*	0.9419	129.83
		(41.37)	(0.000092)		
2.	Sulphur Dioxide (So_2)	166.85**	0.0015*	0.9420	129.82
		(60.69)	(0.0001)		
3.	Oxides of Nitrogen (NO_x)	22.57**	0.0002*	0.9420	129.85
		(8.21)	(0.000018)		
4.	Hydrocarbons (HC)	1.17**	0.00001*	0.9412	128.93
		(0.4241)	(0.0000009)		
5.	Carbon Monoxide (Co)	6.23**	0.00005*	0.9419	129.76
		(2.265)	(0.000005)		

Source: Survey Data.

Note: ** Significant at 5 per cent level.
* Significant at 1 per cent level.
(Figures in brackets refer to the Standard Error)

In air pollution load under different categories namely particulates, sulphur dioxide, oxides of nitrogen, hydrocarbons and carbon monoxide, the co-efficient of determination is 94 per cent which denotes that 94 per cent of the variation, that is, air pollution load has been explained by the independent variable, that is, output in soap industry. This model explains the satisfactory level of variation in 'Y', signifying air pollution load.

In the soap industry, an increase of output by one tonne leads to produce air pollution loads, under different categories, of 1 kg, 1.5 kg, 0.2 kg, 0.01 kg, and 0.05 kg of particulates, sulphur dioxide, oxides of nitrogen, hydrocarbons and carbon monoxide respectively.

Comparing the influence of output and air pollution load under different categories in the soap industry, it is observed that sulpur dioxide is heavier than particulates which in turn is heavier than oxides of nitrogen. The remaining air pollution load namely hydrocarbons and carbon monoxide are in small quantities.

Comparing the influence of output and air pollution load in the soap industry and the cotton-dyeing industry, it is observed that air pollution load is heavy in the cotton-dyeing industry. An increase of one tonne in output leads to 1 kg of particulates in the soap industry, but 11.1 kg, in the cotton-dyeing industry. Similarly it leads to 1.5 kg and 6.3 kg of sulphur dioxide in the two industries respectively. The reason is that more quantity of firewood is required to produce output in the cotton-dyeing industry than in the other industry. Firewood of 0.9 kg, 0.5 kg and 0.9 kg is used to produce 1 kg of output in direct dyes, naphthol dyes and vat dyes respectively in the cotton-dyeing industry, whereas 0.1 kg of firewood is used to produce 1 kg of output in the oil soap manufacturing unit.

ANOVA Model : Variation in Air Pollution Load in three Types of Cotton-Dyeing Industry

An analysis of variance is made in order to examine air pollution load, which varies in the three types of cotton-dyeing industry namely naphthol dyes, vat dyes and direct dyes. Table 7.3 indicates the total level and the average level of particulates in the three types of cotton-dyeing industry.

Table 3

Total and average levels of particulates in three types of cotton-dyeing industry

Sl. No.	*Name of the three types*	*Total for all units (in grams)*	*Average per unit (in grams)*
1.	Naphthol dyes	1134.16	378.05
2.	Vat dyes	90643.52	22660.88
3.	Direct dyes	8463.42	1209.06

Source: Survey Data.

The one way anova of air pollution load gives results, as shown in Tables 4, 6, 8, 10 and 12.

Table 4 refers to the ANOVA of air pollution load of particulates in the cotton-dyeing industry.

Table 4

Anova Of Air Pollution Load In Cotton-dyeing Industry - Particulates

Sources of Variation	*Sum of Squares*	*DF*	*Mean Square*	*F*	*Significant F*
Between types of dyeing	1346989332.96	2	673494666.48	10.963	0.002
Within types	675745247.124	11	61431386.102	—	—
Total	2022734580.09	13	155594967.70	—	—

Source: Survey Data.

The result Table 3 shows that there is a significant difference in air pollution load, particulates, among the three types of cotton-dyeing units. Among the three types, vat dyes have the greatest average particulates load, direct dyes have lesser average particulates load and the naphthol dyes occupy the third place.

Table 5 explains the total and average levels of sulphur dioxide in the three types of cotton-dyeing industry.

Table 7.5

Total and Average Levels of Sulphur Dioxide In the three types of Cotton-dyeing Industry

Sl. No.	*Name of the three types*	*Total for all units (in grams)*	*Average per unit (in grams)*
1.	Naphthol Dyes	1663.99	554.66
2.	Vat Dyes	132987.85	33246.96
3.	Direct Dyes	12417.12	1773.87

Source: Survey Data.

The anova of air pollution load of sulphur dioxide in cotton-dyeing units is given in Table 6.

Table 7.6

Anova of Air Pollution Load In Cotton-dyeing Units - Sulphur Dioxide

Sources of Variation	*Sum of Squares*	*DF*	*Mean Square*	*F*	*Significant F*
Between Types of Dyeing	2899442926.34	2	1449721463.2	10.963	0.002
Within Types	1454566447.81	11	132233313.44	—	—
Total	4354009374.15	13	334923798.01	—	—

Source: Survey Data.

The result Table 5 reveals that there is a significant difference in the air pollution load of sulphur dioxide among the three types of cotton-dyeing industry. Vat dyes have the heaviest air pollution load of sulphur dioxide as for as the average level is concerned. Direct dyes have lesser average level of sulphur dioxide. Naphthol dyes have the lowest air pollution load of sulphur dioxide.

Table 7 highlights the total and average levels of oxides of nitrogen.

Table 7

Total And Average Levels of Oxides of Nitrogen In The Three Types of Cotton-dyeing Industry

Sl. No.	*Name of the three types*	*Total for all units (in grams)*	*Average per unit (in grams)*
1.	Naphthol Dyes	225.17	75.06
2.	Vat Dyes	17996.29	4499.07
3.	Direct Dyes	1680.32	240.05

Source: Survey Data.

Table 8 indicates the anova of air pollution load of oxides of nitrogen in cotton-dyeing industry.

Table 8

Anova Of Air Pollution Load of Oxides of Nitrogen In The Cotton-dyeing Industry

Sources of Variation	*Sum of Squares*	*DF*	*Mean Square*	*F*	*Significant F*
Between Types of Dyeing	53095378.482	2	26547689.241	10.963	0.002
Within Types	26636368.564	11	2421488.051	—	—
Total	79731747.046	13	6133211.311	—	—

Source: Survey Data.

Table 7 indicates that there is a significant difference in air pollution load of oxides of nitrogen among the three types of cotton-dyeing units. Vat dyes have the heaviest load of average level of oxides of nitrogen, direct dyes have lesser load and naphthol dyes have the lowest load of average level of oxides of nitrogen.

Table 9 gives the total and average levels of hydrocarbons.

Table 9

Total And Average Levels of Hydrocarbons In The Three Types of Cotton-dyeing Industry

Sl. No.	*Name of the three types*	*Total for all units (in grams)*	*Average per unit (in grams)*
1.	Naphthol Dyes	11.6	3.87
2.	Vat Dyes	926.37	231.59
3.	Direct Dyes	86.5	12.36

Source: Survey Data.

Table 10 Indicates The Anova of Air Pollution Load of Hydrocarbons In The Cotton-dyeing Units.

Table 10

Anova Of Air Pollution Load Of Hydrocarbons In The Cotton-dyeing Industry

Sources of Variation	*Sum of Squares*	*DF*	*Mean Square*	*F*	*Significant F*
Between Types of Dyeing	140687.035	2	70343.517	10.963	0.002
Within Types	70577.883	11	6416.171	—	—
Total	211264.918	13	16251.148	—	—

Source: Survey Data.

From this analysis it is inferred that there is significant difference in air pollution load of hydrocarbons among the three types of cotton-dyeing units.

Vat dyes have the heaviest load of average level of hydrocarbons, direct dyes have lesser load and naphthol dyes have the lowest load of average level of hydrocarbons.

Table 11 shows the total and average levels of carbon monoxide.

Table 11

Total And Average Levels of Carbon Monoxide In The Three Types of Cotton-dyeing Units

Sl. No.	*Name of the three types*	*Total for all units (in grams)*	*Average per unit (in grams)*
1.	Naphthol dyes	62.09	20.70
2.	Vat dyes	4962.32	1240.58
3.	Direct dyes	463.33	66.19

Source: Survey Data.

Table 12 shows the anova of air pollution load of carbon monoxide in the cotton-dyeing industry.

Table 12

Anova of Air Pollution Load of Carbon Monoxide In The Cotton-dyeing Units

Sources of Variation	*Sum of Squares*	*DF*	*Mean Square*	*F*	*Significant F*
Between Types of Dyeing	4037406.625	2	2018703.312	10.965	0.002
Within Types	2025178.043	11	184107.095	—	—
Total	6062584.668	13	466352.667	—	—

Source: Survey Data.

It is inferred from Table 12 that there is a significant difference in air pollution load of carbon monoxide among the three types of cotton-dyeing units.

Vat dyes have got the heaviest load of average level of carbon monoxide, direct dyes have lesser load and naphthol dyes have the lowest load of average level of carbon monoxide.

It is observed that the air pollution load among the three types of cotton-dyeing industry may vary due to the levels of output also. In order to examine this, the air pollution load under different categories are converted into the load for 1000 kg of output and then the anova model is made. The result reveals that there is no significant difference in air pollution load under different categories among the three types of cotton-dyeing industry.

Simple bar diagrams are drawn to know which types of cotton-dyeing industry produce low or high levels of air pollution load. The results have also been shown in the accompanying Figures 1, 2, 3, 4 and 5.

1. Particulates
2. Sulphur dioxide
3. Oxides of Nitrogen
4. Hydrocarbons
5. Carbon monoxide

It is observed that cotton-dyeing industry has higher load of air pollution and the soap manufacturing industry has lower load of air pollution. The reason is that more quantity of firewood is required to produce output in cotton-dyeing industry than in soap manufacturing industry. Among the three types of cotton-dyeing industry vat dyes produce the highest level of air pollution. Direct dyes produce lesser level of air pollution and naphthol dyes produce still lesser level of air pollution. The reason is in the case of vat dyes, hot water is used to prepare chemical solution. In the case of naphthol dyes, cool water is used to prepare chemical solution. In the case of direct dyes, warm water is used. Energy sources that produce lesser degree of air pollution load should be used in the industries. Air pollution control technology should be adopted in order to minimise or prevent air pollution.

Figure 1
Average Level of Particulars In Cotton-dyeing

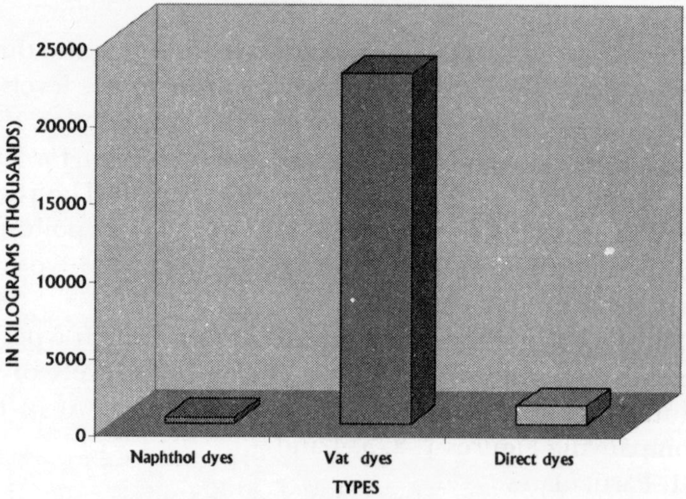

Figure 2
Average Level of Sulphur Dioxide In Cotton-dyeing

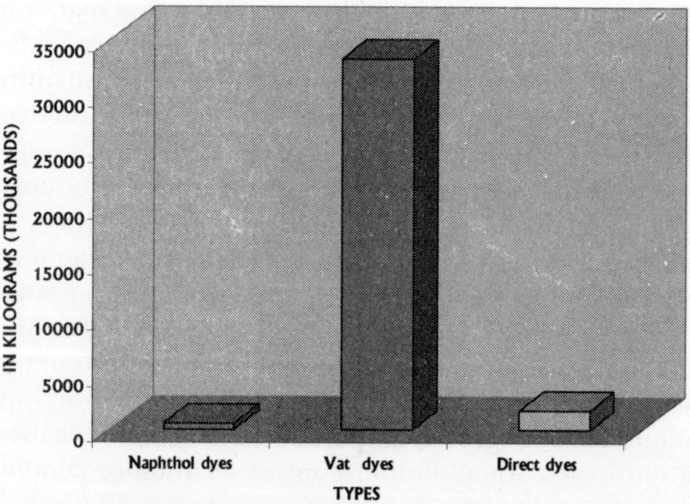

Figure 3
Average Level of
Oxides of Nitrogen In Cotton-dyeing

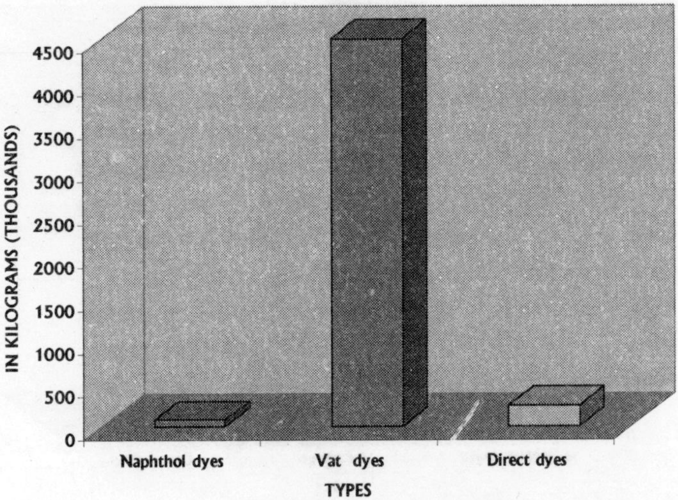

Figure 4
Average Level of
Hydrocarbons In Cotton-dyeing

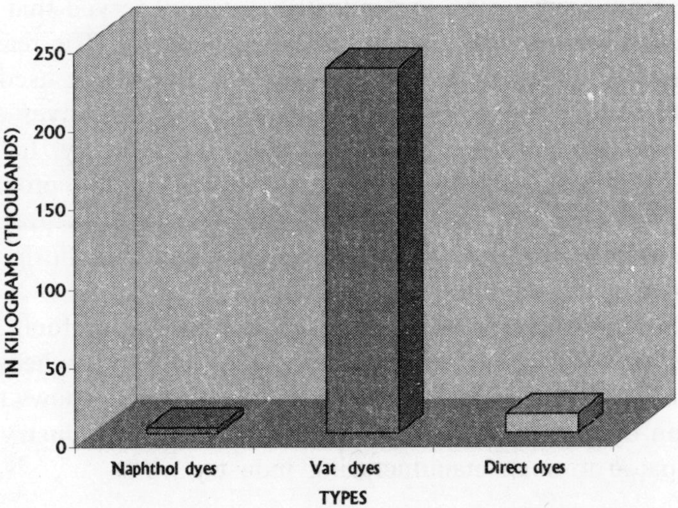

Figure 5
Average Level of
Carbonmonoxide In Cotton-dyeing

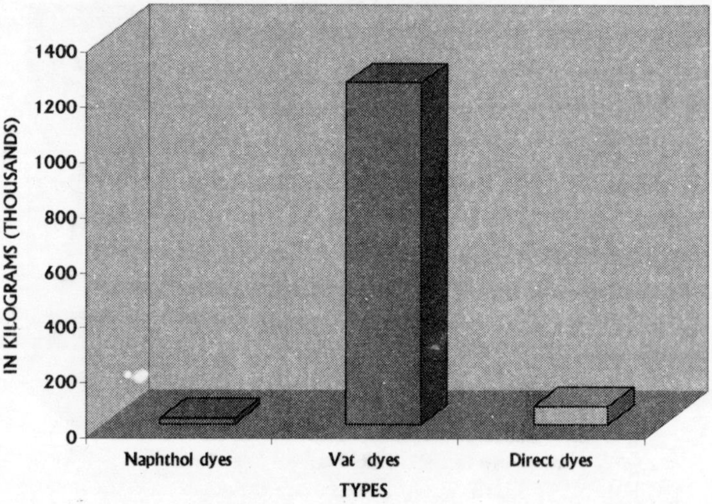

TESTING OF HYPOTHESIS

Comparing the influence of output and air pollution load in soap and cotton-dyeing industries, it is observed that air pollution load is heavy in cotton-dyeing industry. The reason is that 0.9 kg., 0.5 kg. and 0.9 kg. of firewood are used to produce, 1 kg. of output in direct dyes, naphthol dyes and vat dyes respectively in the cotton-dyeing industry. In the case of oil soap industry, 0.1 kg of firewood is used to produce 1 kg. of output. Thus it is seen that firewood is greatly responsible for the air pollution generated in both the industries.

In cotton-dyeing industry, firewood is used as fuel. Air pollution load, produced by cotton-dyeing industry is heavier than that of soap manufacturing industry. Table 13 shows that cotton-dyeing industry is a major air polluting industry as compared to soap manufacturing industry.

Table 13

Air Pollution Load Generated By The Firewood of Fourteen Cotton-dyeing And Ten Soap Manufacturing Units In Madurai District

Aggregate (In Kg)

Sl. No.	*Name of the Industry*	*Fire-wood*	*Out put*	*Parti-culates*	*Salpur dioxide So_2*	*Oxides Nitrogen NO_2*	*Hydro-carbons HC*	*Carbon-monoxide Co*
1.	Soap Industry	405600	4213000	5556.77	8152.62	1103.24	56.79	304.21
		(40560)	(421300)	(555.68)	(815.26)	(110.32)	(5.68)	(30.42)
2.	Cotton-dyeing Industry	7316807	8401619	100241.100	147068.94	19901.77	1024.47	5487.75
		(522629.07)	(600115.64)	(7160.08)	(10504.92)	(1421.56)	(73.18)	(391.98)

Source: Survey Data.

Note: Figures In Brackets Refer To The Average Level.

Air pollution load is heavy in the industries that use firewood as their fuel compared to industries that use kerosene as their fuel. In the cotton-dyeing industry which uses firewood as its fuel, the average levels of air pollution under different categories are 7160.08 kg. of particulates, 10,504.92 kg. of sulphur dioxide, 1,421.56 kg. of oxides of nitrogen, 73.18 kg. of hydrocarbons and 391.98 kg. of carbon monoxide. In the cotton-dyeing industry which uses kerosene as its fuel, the average levels of air pollution under different categories are 2.97 kg. of particulates, 16.83 kg. of sulphur dioxide, 2.28 kg. of oxides of nitrogen, 0.4 kg. of hydrocarbons and 0.25 kg. of carbon monoxide. So it is evident that air pollution in these industries is mainly due to firewood used as fuel. Facts derived from the above analysis indicate that the hypothesis stands proved.

Firewood used as fuel, generates air pollution load on the one side and causes deforestation on the other. In the present study it is observed that approximately 7,722.4 tonnes of firewood are used per year by the sample units of both cotton-dyeing and soap manufacturing industries. Since the average weight of a big tree is three tonnes, it is approximately calculated that in every year 2,574 trees are cut and used resulting in deforestation. Growing trees inside the factories is one method to control air pollution as the trees release oxygen by taking in carbon dioxide.

NOTES

1. T. N. Khoshoo, Environmental Concerns and Strategies, Ashish Publishing House, New Delhi, 1988, p.192.
2. A. V. Munim, "Combating Air Pollution - Mission Impossible?", Chemical Engineering World, Vol. VII, No. 11, November, 1972, p. 38.
3. Howard E. Hesketh, Understanding and Controlling Pollution, Ann Arbor Science Publishers Inc., Michigan, USA, 1973, p. 2.
4. Biman Basu, "Environment Protection: A Many Faceted Problem," Current Topics, Ambala Cantt, July 1986, p. 474.
5. Wilfrid Bach, Atmospheric Pollution, McGraw-Hill Book Comp any, New York, 1989, p. 5.
6. T. N. Khoshoo, "Air pollution and Plants", (Ed.) I. Mohan, Environmental Pollution and Management, Ashish Publishing House, New Delhi, 1989, p.168.
7. Yogendra N. Srivastava, Environmental Pollution, Ashish Publishing house, New Delhi, 1989, p. 16.
8. Inderjeet Sethi, M. S.Sethi and S. A. Sethi, Environmental Pollution, Causes, Effects and Control, Air Pollution and Human Health, Commonwealth Publishers, New Delhi, 1991, p.173.
9. D.N. Rao, P. K. Nandi and M. Agarwal, "Impact of Air Pollution on Urban and Rural Areas," Edited by Pramod Singh, Ecology of Rural India, Ashish Publishing House, New Delhi, 1987, p. 85.

8

Environmental Effects of Pollutants of Small Scale Industries on the Workers and the Household

This chapter consists of two parts. The first part deals with the analysis of the environmental impact of various effluents on the workers employed in small scale units such as electroplating, cotton-dyeing, paint, soap and chemical manufacture. It also deals with the various occupational health hazards of workers as well as the availability of medical facilities for them. The second part deals with the environmental effects on the members of the household, who are living nearby the polluting industries.

Environmental health refers to the ecological balance that must exist between man and his environment in order to ensure his well-being. The deterioration of the human environment through population explosion, pollution of air and water, and other disruptions of the ecological balance pose a major international health hazard and a serious challenge. J. Logan, in his paper published in the 'American Journal of Tropical Medicine' in 1960, points out that environmentally transmitted diseases are reaponsible for the sufferings of 500 million people every year, particularly infants and children.[1]

The U.N. Secretary General's report on the problem of human environment sounds a similar ominous note. "If current trends continue, the failure of life on earth could be engendered and thus, it is urgent to focus world attention on these problems which threaten humanity in an environment that permits the realisation of the highest human aspirations".[2]

"Health is a state of dynamic equilibrium between an organism and its environment in which all functions of mind and body are normal".[3]

The health status of an individual, a community or a nation is determined by the interplay and integration of two ecological universes, the internal environment within man himself and the external environment which surrounds him. The industrial worker today is placed in a highly complicated environment which is getting more complicated as man is becoming more ingenious.

The whole environment of a man could be classified as: the working environment in the community and home environment. Among these, the working environment has direct effects on the health of the persons who are present in the area. The environment may be responsible in the causation of occupational diseases or in exacerbation of other non-occupational diseases. The state of health of the worker can influence his ability to work safely and efficiently.

The environmental factors, such as the presence of contaminants in the air, physical factors like heat, humidity, noise and radiation, concentration of substances like metals, pesticides, dyes, gases and fumes have an impact on the state of health of the workers. Workers, exposed to all these toxic agents are at the risk of suffering from their harmful effects. It is, therefore, of vital importance that the employees who are required to work in industries should be protected and kept in a healthy state.

It is estimated that every three minutes one worker dies of an occupational injury or illness and every second at least three workers are injured in the world. Every year 1.8 lakh workers die and 11 crores get injured in occupational accidents.[4] The question of occupational hazards is related to a number of factors such as the nature of technology used, the organisation of production, the provision of services, the pursuit of profit and the capacity of the workers to protect themselves. The employment opportunities are shrinking in the organised sector. This will result in thousands of potential workers fighting for fewer jobs and thus becoming less able to defend themselves against hazards introduced by newer technologies.[5]

The unorganised sector usually employs hazard- prone, labour-oriented technology and the workers are not skilled either. Since the workers in this sector do not usually come under the purview of any legislation or labour laws, the working conditions depend upon the employers' financial resources and attitude towards their workers. Unregulated work hours, low wages and the virtual absence of health, welfare and hygiene facilities add to the misery of the workers.[6]

Development of Small Scale Industries, based purely on economic considerations, without taking environmental or societal dimensions into account, have often resulted in outright erosion of human rights. Even the basic and fundamental rights to live, to economically prosper and to develop are endangered.

Discharge of toxic wastes and emissions from Small Scale Industries at times result in permanent damage to the environment. There are many Small Scale Industries engaged in mining activities, which have displaced the local people and have inflicted tremendous harm on their health and well-being. In fact in a mining village, there is not a single household without a widow and nobody there has ever lived longer than 40 Years of age.[7]

OCCUPATIONAL HEALTH HAZARDS - PROBLEMS OF WORKERS

Health of a worker is also influenced by the age and his service period. Continuous service for a longer period produces some deterimental effects on the worker's health.

Totally sixty four workers have been taken as sample. Statistical data regarding the incidence of occupational diseases caused by the effluents of chemical product industry, electroplating industry, cotton-dyeing industry, paint industry and soap industry have been collected. The associated population revealed that the workers suffered from various diseases, particularly tuberculosis, stomach pain, suffocation, cold and cough, ulcer, skin problems, eye irritation, ear problem, sore throat, asthma, head ache and bronchitis.

To find out the type and nature of occupational diseases 64 workers were taken as sample and studied.

The number of sample respondents suffering from some diseases or problems is shown in Table 1.

Table 1
The Number of Sample Workers Suffering From Occupational Diseases

Sl.	*Name of The Industry*	*Sufferers*	*Free From Suffering*	*Total Sample*
1.	Chemical Product	6	4	10
2.	Electroplating	5	5	10
3.	Cotton-dyeing	10	10	20
4.	Paint	6	2	8
5.	Soap	10	6	16
	Total	37	27	64

Source: Survey Data.

Table 1 reveals that out of 64 sample respondents taken for study, only 27 (42.2 per cent) workers are found to be free from any illness. Of the 8 samples taken from the paint industry, six suffer from some illness. Next to that, 10 soap industry workers are affected, while 6 are free. It is found that 6 workers of chemical product, 5 of electroplating and 10 of cotton-dyeing industries suffer from some illness. Nearly fifty-eight per cent of the workers in all these industries have been affected by various diseases.

In order to find out the type of diseases affecting the workers in different polluting industries, an attempt was made to explain all polluting industries one by one.

Table 2 shows the different diseases with which the workers of the chemical product industry are frequently affected.

Table 2

Different Diseases Found Among The Workers of The Chemical Product Industry

Tuberculosis	*Stomach Pain*	*Suffocation*	*Cold*	*Ulcer*	*Skin Problem*	*Total*
1	1	1	1	1	1	6

Source: Survey Data.

Sixty per cent of the workers of the chemical industry are affected by various diseases. Workers suffering from tuberculosis, stomach pain, suffocation, frequent cold, ulcer or skin problems are found to be one in each (16.67 per cent). The remaining 40 per cent of the workers are free from any serious ailment.

Most of the workers do not have any other source of income. Hence they have to spend from their monthly salary for their medical expenses.

Details of the total number of workers who are members of the Employees State Insurance (ESI) and others who meet the medical expenses from their monthly salary are presented in Table 3.

Table 3
Details of Medical Care

Members of Esi	*Private Medical Care*	*Total*
—	3	3

Source: Survey Data.

The factories which have less than 13 workers do not become members of the E.S.I. As the selection of the sample units are Small Scale Industries, they have limited workers. The owners of the chemical factories do not provide medical facilities for their workers through E.S.I. hospitals. Fifty per cent of them go to private nursing homes for treatment. Others do not take their illness very seriously.

Table 4 indicates the different diseases with which the electroplating industry workers are frequently affected.

Table 4
Different Diseases Found Among the Workers of the Electroplating Industry

Cold And Cough	*Dermatitis*	*Sore Throat*	*Ear Problem*	*Ulcer*
2	1	1	1	5

Source: Survey Data.

Fifty per cent of the electroplating industry workers are free from any serious ailment. Among the remaining workers, forty per cent suffer from cold and cough, twenty per cent from dermatitis, twenty per cent from sore throat and twenty per cent from ear problem which is due to the noise created by the machines. The affected workers are all above thrity years and they have put in more than ten years of service.

Details of medical care taken by the electroplating industry workers are presented in Table 5.

Table 8.5
Details of Medical Care

Members of The E.S.I.	*Private Medical Care*	*Total*
—	1	1

Source: Survey Data.

The workers in electroplating industry cannot afford to get treatment in the E.S.I hospitals. Twenty per cent of them are financially sound enough to get treatment in private nursing homes. The remaining eighty per cent are unable to get medical treatment facilities either from E.S.I hospitals or from private nursing homes.

Table 6 represents the different diseases with which the cotton-dyeing industry workers are frequently affected.

Table 6
Different Diseases Found Among The Workers of The Cotton-dyeing Industry

Suffocation	*Cold And Cough*	*Asthma*	*Total*
4	1	5	10

Source: Survey Data.

Table 6 reveals that out of twenty sample respondents taken for study purpose, only ten workers are found to be free from any illness. Among the remaining workers, forty per cent suffer from suffocation, ten per cent from cold and cough and fifty per cent from asthma.

Details of medical care taken by the cotton-dyeing industry workers are given in Table 7.

Table 7
Details of Medical Care

Members of The E.S.I.	Private Medical Care	Total
—	7	7

Source: Survey Data.

The factory owners do not provide medical facilities for their workers through E.S.I hospitals. Seventy per cent of them are financially sound to get treatment in private nursing homes. The remaining thirty per cent are unable to get treatment either from the E.S.I hospitals or from private nursing homes.

Table 8 shows the different diseases with which the paint industry workers are frequently affected.

Table 8
Different Diseases Found Among The Workers of the Paint Industry

Head Ache	*Eye Irritation*	*Stomach Pain*	*Ulcer*	*Bronchitis*	*Total*
1	2	1	1	1	6

Source: Survey Data.

Table 8 shows that seventy-five per cent of the paint industry workers suffer from different diseases- 16.67 per cent of the workers suffer from headache, 33.3 per cent from eye irritation, 16.67 per cent from stomach pain, 16.67 per cent from ulcer and 16.67 per cent from Bronchitis. The remaining 25 per cent of the workers are free from any diseases.

Details of medical care taken by the paint industry workers are presented in Table 9.

Table 9
Details of Medical Care

Members Of The E.s.i	*Private Medical Care*	*Total*
—	2	2

Source: Survey Data.

Table 9 reveals that 33.3 per cent of the workers get treatment in private nursing homes. The remaining 66.7 per cent are unable to get treatment either from the E.S.I hospitals or from private nursing homes.

Table 10 represents the different diseases with which the soap industry workers are frequently affected.

Table 10

Different Diseases Found Among The Workers of the Soap Industry

Suffocation	*Stomach pain*	*Ulcer*	*Dermatitis*	*Total*
2	4	3	1	10

Source: Survey Data.

37.5 per cent of the soap industry workers are free from any ailment. Among the remaining workers, twenty per cent suffer from suffocation, forty per cent from stomach pain, thirty per cent from ulcer and ten per cent from dermatitis.

Table 11 presents details of medical care taken by the soap industry workers.

Table 11

Details of Medical Care

Members Of The E.S.I.	*Private Medical Care*	*Total*
—	4	4

Source: Survey Data.

The factory owners do not offer medical facilities for their workers through the E.S.I hospitals. Forty per cent of them are financially sound to get treatment in private nursing homes. The remaining sixty per cent are unable to get treatment either from the E.S.I hospitals or from private nursing homes.

Table 12 presents details of the percentage of workers of various polluting industries who are affected by different occuptional diseases.

Table 12

The Percentage of Workers In The Polluting Industries Affected By Occupational Diseases (1991-92)

Sl. No. — Name of the Industry — Number of Workers Affected By Occupational Diseases (%)

Sl. No.	*Name of the Industry*	*Number of Workers Affected Occupational Diseases (%)*
1.	Chemical Industry	60.0
2.	Electroplating Industry	50.0
3.	Cotton-dyeing Industry	50.0
4.	Paint Industry	75.0
5.	Soap Industry	62.5

Source: Survey Data.

Seventy five per cent of the paint industry workers, 62.5 per cent of the soap industry workers, sixty per cent of the chemical industry workers, fifty per cent of the cotton-dyeing industry workers and fifty per cent of the electroplating industry workers are affected by different occupational diseases.

Table 13 presents the nature and types of diseases of the sample workers of the various polluting Small Scale Industries.

Table 13 presents the fact that among all the workers in various polluting industries, 18.92 per cent suffer from suffocation, 16.22 per cent suffer from stomach pain, 13.51 per cent from ulcer, 13.51 per cent from asthma, 10.81 per cent from cold and cough, 8.11 per cent from dermatitis, 5.41 per cent from eye irritation, 2.7 per cent from tuberculosis, 2.7 per cent from headache, 2.7 per cent from bronchitis and 2.7 per cent from ear problem.

In the case of chemical, paint and soap industries, the workers are affected by various occupational diseases,

Table 13

Nature And Types of Diseases of the Sample Workers (1991-92)

Name of the Industry	*Tuber-culosis*	*Stomach pain*	*Suffo-cation*	*Cold and cough*	*Ulcer*	*Derma-titis (or) skin problem*	*Eye irri-tation*	*Sore throat*	*Asthma*	*Head-ache*	*Bron-chi-tis*	*Ear Problem*	*Total*
Chemical Product	1 (16.67)	1 (16.67)	1 (16.67)	1 (16.67)	1 (16.67)	1 (16.67)	—	—	—	—	—	—	6
Electro- plating	—	—	—	2 (40.00)	—	1 (20.00)	—	1 (20.00)	—	—	—	1 (20.00)	5
Cotton-Dyeing	—	—	4 (40.00)	1 (10.00)	—	—	—	—	5 (50.00)	—	—	—	10
Paint	—	1 (16.67)	—	—	1 (16.67)	—	2 (33.31)	—	—	1 (16.67)	1 (16.67)	—	6
Soap	—	4 (40.00)	2 (20.00)	—	3 (30.00)	1 (10.00)	—	—	—	—	—	—	10
Grand Total	1 (2.70)	6 (16.22)	7 (18.92)	4 (10.81)	5 (13.51)	3 (8.11)	2 (5.41)	1 (2.70)	5 (13.51)	1 (2.70)	1 (2.70)	1 (2.70)	37

Source: Survey Data.

Note: Figures in brackets indicate percentage.

irrespective of any particular age or service period. But in the case of electroplating and cotton-dyeing industries, the workers who have put in more than ten years of service and are above thirty years are only affected by different occupational diseases.

ENVIRONMENTAL EFFECTS ON THE HOUSEHOLD

The industrial waste water pollutes the entire surroundings in which the factory is situated. Especially the waste water produced by the cotton-dyeing units and electroplating units affect the entire households around. But in the case of paint, soap and chemical product industries, the waste water pollution is not much. In order to assess the waste water pollution, members of eighteen families living nearby the cotton-dyeing units at Avaniapuram and Villapuram were interviewed. They make use of well water and water from the borewells for general purposes, but they rely upon the municipal water supply for drinking water. During the rainy season, well water and the borewell water become extremely salty or bitter in taste. This is so because, the industrial waste water flows into the ditches nearby. During the summer season, since the water gets evaporated, the chemicals that are mixed in the waste water of the cotton-dyeing units become sediments and when the rain falls, these chemicals get mixed with the rain water and sink into the ground. This underground water tastes very salty, thus affecting the quality of potable water.

Out of ten families, seven families are residing at Jaihindpuram, where the concentration of the electroplating industry is high. Almost all the respondents have accepted that there is definitely an impact of the waste water of the electroplating units with respect to the negative change in the environment.

The foul smell of the waste water let out during the evenings by the electroplating units causes much hardship both to the young and old members of the families living nearby. To avoid the suffocation due to the bad odour of the lime and acid wastes, all the family members of the surrounding areas have to keep themselves shut up inside the houses. The wooden panels of the windows and the walls of the houses are affected by the acid particles of the industrial waste water.

Even the lime coating on the walls is affected due to this waste water pollution.

ENVIRONMENTAL EFFECTS ON THE AGRICULTURAL LAND

Since there is no agricultural land nearby these polluting units, such as cotton-dyeing and electroplating, the farmers are not affected. Also the waste water does not cause any damage to the agricultural lands situated away from these units, since the polluted water does not run through and mix with the lake water used for agricultural purposes. The industrial waste water runs into and mixes with the public sewage.

It is clear that Small Scale Industries provide employment opportunity at a maximum level. At the same time it is quite true that they create occupational health hazards to their workers. The factory owners should provide medical facilities for their workers or medical allowances should be given to them for taking immediate medical treatment. If the factories fail to do this, then the Government should provide medical facilities to the workers under the labour welfare programmes.

The environment can be considered an integral part of health development, since any impact on man's environment influences his state of well-being. Every sector of the nation's economy, while trying to develop, leaves its impact on environment and therefore every sector or department of the economy, while planning for its growth, should at the same time pay adequate attention to the negative impact on environment and take simultaneous steps by devising suitable strategies to minimise and if possible totally eliminate consequent health degradation due to environmental pollution.

NOTES

1. WHO, World Health, May 1972, p.28.
2. U. Thant quoted in M. C. Clellan, and S. Grant (ed), Protecting Our Environments, New York, 1970, p. 206.
3. Daniel N. Lapedes, Dictionary of Scientific and Technical Terms, Mc-Graw Hill Publishers, 2nd Edition, New York, 1978, p. 58.
4. Arun kumar Bhatt, "Dangerous work", The Hindu, Survey of the Environment, 1993, p. 84.
5. Dunu Roy, "Occupational Hazards, When the Grind Tells on You," The Hindu, Survey of the Environment, 1993, p. 80.
6. Arun Kumar Bhatt, Op.Cit, p. 85.
7. K. P. Nyati, Problems of Pollution and its control in Small Scale Industries, Friedrich Ebert Stiftung Foundation, New Delhi, 1988, p.10.

9

Pollution Control Measures

INTRODUCTION

Industries and their products have an impact on the 'environment'. The entire cycle of raw material exploration, its transformation into the final product, the energy consumed in the process, the disposal of wastes, and the marketing of the product - all these affect man and society in some way or the other. Industrialisation results in positive effect (production of goods) as well as negative effect (degradation of environment and depletion of resources). Industrial pollution is the basic problem having adverse effect on the health and safety of not only the industrial workers, but also of the residents of that area. This problem is more acute in big cities and industrial towns.[1]

Economic development and environmental protection must go hand in hand. They are the two sides of the same coin. One cannot be sacrificed for the sake of the other. For both, technological development is necessary. Environmental pollution control requires at least the technology as much advanced as which brings in economic development but at the same time it should minimise the pollution of environment as its bye-product. Growth must be balanced with a due regard for maintaining environmental quality through an 'eco-development plan'. Such a plan will imply a planned development based on the principle that 'an economy is part of a larger eco- system'. This will include a co-ordinated management of the economy and the protection of air, water and land resources, which are polluted by development activities.

The cost of coping with pollution problems are going to be tremendous. "Environmental pollution is not an incidental bye-product; rather it is an intrinsic feature of every technology developed to enhance productivity. This technology is so imbedded in the agricultural and industrial production processes that the required change would involve serious economic dislocations".[2]

In the early decades of industrial pollution, industry resisted all efforts at pollution control, as money spent on pollution control would diminish profit and capitalist economy was most concerned with profits.

But this attitude underwent a change in the fifties and the sixties. Where an industry felt that it could afford to implement pollution controls and still make sufficient profit to maintain expansion and research, it was willing to spend money voluntarily on pollution control, but where it was at the cost of profitability, no voluntary action on pollution control was taken. Sometimes an industry is found engaged much more in image-building than in genuine pollution control.[3]

HISTORY OF ENVIRONMENT POLICY IN INDIA

Policy formulation

Environmental policy formulation in India dates back to the Stockholm Conference of 1972 wherein developed countries visualised the environmental problem as an affliction of industrialisation and suggested no growth policy as the only viable means of protecting the biosphere. The developing countries including India, shared the view that their environmental problems are mostly due to lack of development rather than excessive development. The Indian Prime Minister stated at the Stockholm conference that the rich countries may look upon development as the cause of environmental destruction, but to us, it is one of the primary means of improving the environment for living, for providing food, water, sanitation, shelter, of making deserts green and mountains habitable.[4]

These views have formed part of the basic environmental philosophy of India and have found expression in various government policy pronouncements. Clearly the objective of environmental policy in India is 'development with conservation'.

Implementation Measures

In February 1972 a National Committee on Environmental Planning and Co-ordination (NCEPC) was set up to plan and co-ordinate environmental programmes and policies and advise various ministeries and government departments on the solution of environmental problems.

In February 1980, the now famous Tiwari Committee was set up. The committee laid great stress on the need to ensure the optimal management of the country's natural resources and recommended the setting up of a central land commission as a first step towards the end.[5]

A major outcome of Tiwari committee recommendation was the creation in November 1980, of a Department of Environment (DOEN) at the Centre to serve, in a co-ordinating role, as a model agency for environmental protection and eco-development. Its aim was to carry out environmental appraisal of development projects and assume direct administrative responsibility for pollution-monitoring and regulation, for the conservation of biosphere reserves, and the conservation of marine eco-systems. The WCEPC was replaced by a National Committee on Environmental Planning (NCEP) in April 1981.

The functions of this Committee were to serve as a think-tank on environment policy matters and provide planning and advisory inputs to DOEN and other Central and State agencies.

Industry and Environment Policy

Environment policy, as related to industry, is implicit in the various pollution control laws and the environmental procedures of the DOEN. Pollution control consists of the legal, institutional, scientific and technological arrangements established to avoid or mitigate excesses in the environment. It can be accomplished by containing pollutants at the source by devising new technologies of manufacture that would eliminate or reduce the production pollutants and enable the industrial units to reuse materials and commodities through reprocessing and resource recovery.

Pollution control does not mean the elimination of all substances put in the air, water or on the land. It is noteworthy that even in the proper use of air and water, impurities get mixed, though only in amounts that permit a renewal of purity.[6]

Legal Regulation of Water Pollution

India is one of the few countries of the world that have made specific reference in the constitution to the need for environmental protection and improvement. Under the Indian Constitution, it is one of the fundamental duties of the state, "to protect and improve environment and to sufeguard the forests and wild life of the country".[7] Besides the State's obligation towards the society at large, the individual members of the society themselves owe a fundamental duty", to protect and improve the natural environment including forests, lakes, rivers and wild life and to have compassion for living creatures. Therefore constitutionally man is required in the process of prosecution of his purposes, to protect and improve the natural environment.[8]

The major comprehensive legislations in India for the prevention and control of water and air pollution are the following:

1. The Water (Prevention and Control of Pollution) Act, 1974.
2. The Water (Prevention and Control of Pollution) Amendment Act, 1978.
3. The Water (Prevention and Control of Pollution) Cess Act, 1977.
4. The Air (Prevention and Control of Pollution) Act, 1981.
5. The Environment Protection Act, 1986.

The Water (prevention and control of pollution) Act, 1974 was passed (amended in 1978) with the following objectives:

1. To provide for the prevention and control of water pollution and maintaining or restoring of wholesomeness of water (in the streams or wells or sewer or on land).
2. To establish Central and State Boards with a view to carrying out the above purposes.
3. For conferring on and assigning to such Boards, powers and functions relating thereto and for matters connected therewith.

This Act resulted in the formation of the Central Board for Prevention and Control of Water Pollution (CBPCWP) with primary duties of setting standards, monitoring and legal enforcement.[9] Further it imposed a prohibition on a person to discharge sewage or trade effluent into a stream without the consent of the Board.[10]

For the contravention of the standards laid down by the State Board and for violation of the provisions relating to the consent by the Board, stiff penalties have been provided. The punishment on conviction will be imprisonment for a term which may extend to three months or fine which may extend to five thousand rupees or both. In the case of continuing failure, the Act provides for a penalty of an additional fine which may extend to one thousand rupees for every day during which such failure continues after the conviction for the first such failure. Penalty for contravention of the provisions of Section 24 shall not be less than six months but it may extend to six years and fine.[11]

As far as the discharge of sewage or trade effluent on land is concerned, the 1978 amendment of the act requires consent orders of the Board. But there is nothing in the Act with regard to storage on land.

Legal Regulation of Air Pollution

To control air pollution, Indian Government has passed. The Air (prevention and control of pollution) Act, 1981. This Act provides for separate Central and State Boards for the prevention and control of air pollution but at present this authority has been granted to the Central and State Water Pollution Prevention Board. The public affected by air pollution cannot approach the courts without prior permission from the Board. This discourages people from participating in the execution of the National Policy.

Section 21(1) of the Air Pollution Act says that no person shall without the previous consent of the State Board, operate any industrial plant specified in the schedule in an air pollution control area.

The recently enacted Environment (Protection) Act, 1986 is the most comprehensive legislation in this field. It covers pollution from solid, liquid and gaseous wastes as well as toxic or hazardous substances. This Act also has many innovations. For example it covers issues related to occupational safety; it allows a citizen to initiate legal proceedings; it has provisions for legal enforcement against Government officials; it has enough flexibility to introduce positive sanctions, and to impart greater participatory role to various interest groups and so on.

It empowers the Central Government to make rules for the maximum allowable limits of concentration of various environmental pollutants for different areas.[12] The penalties for the defaulters have been made more stringent. This Act provides for the imprisonment of the defaulters for upto a total of seven years and or fine which may extend upto Rs. One lakh.[13]

TAMIL NADU POLLUTION CONTROL BOARD

The main functions of the Tamil Nadu Pollution Control Board are

1. To plan a comprehensive programme for the prevention and control of the abatement of pollution of water and land for the prevention and control or the abatement of air pollution in the state.
2. To encourage, conduct and participate in investigation and research, relating to problems of water, land and air pollution and prevention and control or abatement of water, land and air pollution.
3. To inspect sewage or trade effluent works and plants for the treatment of sewage or trade effluent and to review plans, specifications or other data relating to plants set up for the treatment of water.
4. To lay down, modify or annul effluent standards for sewage or trade effluent and for the quality of receiving water resulting from the discharge of effluents and to classify water of the state and to evolve standards for emissions from industries and automobiles.

The Board collects samples of effluent from industries before and after treatment to assess the adequacy of treatment measures. The Board also has launched prosecution against 14 industrial units for not treating the effluent to the standards prescribed by the Board.

Well-equipped laboratories are an important requirement for the Tamil Nadu Pollution Control Board to monitor air and water quality throughout the State. The Board's control laboratory at Madras was strengthened by the acquisition of several sophisticated instruments. A regional laboratory has been set up at Madurai and one more regional laboratory is under establishment at Salem. The Board participates in the National Ambient Air Quality Monitoring Programmme in collaboration with the Central Board for the Prevention and Control of Water Pollution, New Delhi. To start with, one station has been established in Kathiwakkam and the air quality is being monitored daily.[14]

Instead of evolving their own standards for domestic and industrial effluent, the Boards more or less follow the standards prescribed by the Indian Standard Institute (ISI). The Central Board follows three standards with minor variations. It has not yet adopted ISI standards for domestic effluent. The State Boards generally follow standards without any variation. ISI has developed standards for industrial effluents, sewage effluents and streams.[15]

Minimal National Standards

To expedite establishment of pollution control in the existing group of industry, the Central Pollution Control Board has evolved an industry - specific pollution control strategy based on the comprehensive industry document. This document presents details of numbers, sizes, geographical distribution, material inputs, processes adopted, product mix, bye-products recovery, water consumption, various waste streams and their characterization. It particularly deals in prevention and control methods of waste water as against their cost implications.

The document evolves the industry -specific Minimal National Standard (MINAS) by evaluating the cost of various levels of treatment. The capital cost on this measure is converted in annuity taking relevant interest on capital and depreciation. This annuity is converted into annual burden by adding operational, maintenance and repair cost for each level of treatment. The level of treatment for which the annual burden remains within three per cent of the turnover is accepted as the appropriate level of treatment, to be installed by each existing specific industry. The concomitant effluent quality is termed MINAS which cannot be relaxed by State Pollution Control Boards. Stricter effluent quality is prescribed if specific location so demands.[16]

POLLUTION CONTROL POLICY INSTRUMENTS

Pollution is likely to be with us in some form or the other since all production involves pollution in one form or another. Zero pollution can be reached only with zero production. The requirement is a package of measures to identify and monitor pollutants, to identify their economic, sociological and ecological effects and to confine them within levels which are not only safe for survival but fully appropriate to the quality of life expected. This involves a choice between two things: economic growth and the carrying capacity of the environment. In fact as Robert Arvill says, "economic considerations are one half of environmental equation - the other is ecological capacity".[17]

Figure 1 illustrates the processes of raw material extraction, processing, manufacture and consumption in the economy and indicates where various policy instruments to discourage waste and encourage waste reduction, recycling and more stringent residuals management could be introduced.[18]

In broad terms, four general methods have been proposed for the control of activities that damage the environment.[19]

1. Moral suasion, which is an appeal to reduce pollution in the broader interests of the society.
2. Regulations requiring polluters to cut back their emissions to maintain a certain level of environmental quality or to install a specified treatment of procedures. It takes two forms. a) imposition of legal ceilings on the amount any polluter is permitted to emit or discharge and b)

Specification of how particular activity must be carried on.

3. Market processes or pricing or fiscal techniques which include:

Figure 1

Pollution Control Policy Instruments

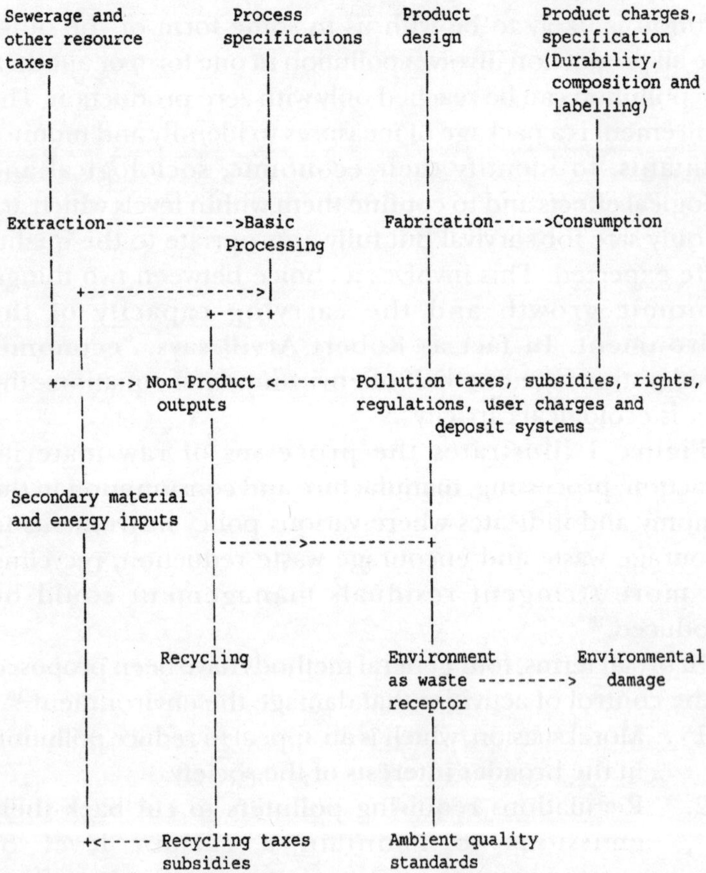

(a) An Effluent Charges or Pollution Taxes

An effluent charges refer to charges of a fixed amount

per unit of waste imposed on all sources of a given kind of waste.

Pollution taxes mean taxes which are levied on the polluters. It is suggested that the polluters should be taxed for the privilege of polluting, so that they may pollute less. A tax on pollution, requires the polluter to install a meter that registers the effluents or emissions released in the production process. In accordance with the level of emissions or effluents, the firm will be charged. Thus higher the level of wastes discharged by a firm, higher will be the tax bill for the firm and a firm can reduce its tax bill by polluting less.

(b) Subsidy

Subsidy means non-repayable forms of financial assistance, contigent on the adoption of pollution abatement measures. It mostly covers a part of the investment on pollution control equipment. The other part of the cost of the equipment is to be borne by the firm. A subsidy is based on the quantity of emissions reduced. It encourages outputs to expand. Thus a subsidy that is intended to reduce pollution actually increases it by causing expansion in the firm's output.

(c) Pollution Permits

Under this the environmental authority determines the maximum amount of a specific type of pollution per unit of time that is within safe limits - that is consistent with the community's environmental objective - and then issues a batch of permits authorising (altogether) just that amount of pollution. Each permit could give its owner the 'right' to pollute upto a specified amount in a given place during a particular period of time. When the impact of pollution varies between locations, number of permits issued in each location can be varied depending on the impact of pollution.[20]

(d) Refundable Deposits

Robert Solow and Edwin Mills have suggested the method of using a refundable deposit for pollution in cases where it is not possible to monitor, observe and detect environmental damage. The potential offenders should be required to leave an appropriate deposit with the environmental authorities which can pay an interest on all such deposits. The funds may be used by the environmental authorities for the environmental protection activities but must be refunded to the polluter in case he ceases his activities that caused pollution. This technique has been found to be very useful in the encouragement of recycling or reuse.

(e) Allocation of Property Rights

It is a method that protects the environmental resources by putting them into the hands of private individuals who consequently have a financial stake in their preservation. Everybody's property is no one's property. Common property resources are over-consumed or exploited. If exclusive property rights are defined for such resources, the public-good environmental quality can be transformed into a private-good and optimal environmental allocation can be reached. Government intervention is needed only in assigning environmental property titles with property rights adequately defined, and the market will find the correct allocation.

4. Government Investment Programmes - These include installation of waste treatment plants, slum clearance, management of wild life, refugees, reforestation and afforestation. Besides these, the research programmes and programmes to create environmental awareness are also part of government investment programmes. There are thus various policy instruments available to control pollution and preserve environmental quality. New methods and concepts are also being developed along with new technologies to control pollution. For efficient management of environment, various combinations of different tools are required.[21]

VOLUNTARY AGENCIES IN ENVIRONMENT MANAGEMENT

It has been realised that the role of citizens in managing environment is important. No government can reach its anticipated level of development, and efficiency cannot by itself solve all environmental problems. The role of non-governmental organisations especially voluntary organisations (both from common people and business communities) is essential in tackling environmental problems. More voluntary organisations are needed to make government's environmental policy very effective.

These voluntary organisations are expected to work with the following objectives:

1. Conservation and development of land, water, air, flora and fauna.
2. Promotion of environmental awareness at all levels by organising seminars and workshops.
3. Tree plantation, involving local people in the tree planting programmes of the government, to mitigate deforestation.
4. To take part in environmental education programmes of the government, especially for women and rural children.

CONTROL OF POLLUTION IN SMALL SCALE INDUSTRIES - THE PROBLEMS

Small Scale Industries despite their higher aggregated pollution potential, are far less equipped individually to resolve their pollution problems. Large and medium size industrial units, generally, do posses the requisite technical, financial and legal capabilities to sort out their pollution problems. The Small Scale Industries however fall exactly on the other end of the spectrum, characterized by lack of information, absence of technical expertise and paucity of financial resources. Small Scale Industries are facing certain problems which could be classified into the following four distinct categories.[22]

INFORMATION POVERTY

Small Scale Industries are neither aware that they are polluting nor they posses the information on legal repercussions if they do not comply with pollution control regulations. Many existing Small Scale Industries exhibit 'could not care more' attitude. It is an indication of lack of information on the legal position of pollution control imperatives.

The agencies like Small Industries Service Institutes and State Industrial Development Corporations which provide all kinds of help, guidance and assitance to potential entrepreneurs, do not even make a mention of pollution control aspects, let alone providing for the cost of pollution control measures in their financial viability computations on the project report. None of the SISIs have any pollution control specialist on their pay role to guide the entrepreneurs. In the last two years not many Small Scale Industries have come forward to claim 50 per cent of the cost of pollution control measures or Rs.50,000 whichever is less, being offered as outright grant or subsidy by the Directorate of Industries, Delhi Administration, to promote control of pollution.

LEGAL PROBLEMS

The Pollution Control Acts require that Small Scale Industries when they are to be set up, should obtain 'No Objection Certificates' (NOCs) from concerned Pollution Control Boards. In NOC application, the entrepreneur is expected to provide details of production, nature of wastes, proposed provision for pollution control, and whether the discharges would affect the surroundings. Collection of such data is not only difficult and expensive, but there is not any institutional mechanism to render such help. Consequently applications are incomplete, resulting either in delay or rejection.

Even when NOCs have been obtained, Small Scale Industries are required to obtain the 'consents' for dicharge of pollutants before commissioning the plant. 'Consents' invariably specify the permissible limits for discharge of various pollutants. These limits are usually based on country-wide generalities and do not reflect specific constraints and problems of an individual unit.

To obtain 'consents', Small Scale Industries are expected to furnish the analysis of waste water or emissions, for which analysis and monitoring facilities particularly in rural and backward areas are lacking.

These 'consents' are renewed every year and in some cases every three years, even though there may not be any change in production capacity or process. Renewal formalities are, therefore, time-consuming and slow.

When the Acts are violated and legal suits are filed, Small Scale Industries tend to prolong the already over-stretched court proceedings to avoid further the burden of additional investment on pollution control measures. Many a time SSI would prefer to prolong the case long enough, until they have exhausted the eligibility period of various fiscal incentives that the Government offers to them. Such a period could be 3 to 5 years. Once that period is over and incentives are withdrawn, they would have closed their shutters down any way due to sudden drop in their profitability. Protracted legal battle for them therefore becomes a cheaper and a viable alternative to installing pollution control equipment. In the meantime pollution goes on unabatted.

Degree of strictness in enforcing these Acts varies from state to state. As a result, a Small Scale Industry, located in a state where there is relative laxity, continues to enjoy competitive advantage over the units which had to invest on pollution control measures. Thus a unit not having pollution control measures tends to produce more as it can sell more, thus creating more pollution.

TECHNO-MANAGERIAL PROBLEMS

Small Scale Industries generally have small plots, sufficient enough to house the production plants. Acquiring additional space for pollution control facilities in many cases may not be possible or may be too expensive.

Technical assistance of knowledgeable consultants is difficult to obtain, as most consultants prefer to work for large and medium industries, where they earn more. Consequently Small Scale Industries are left with 'Fly-by-night' consultants resulting in temporary or sub-optimal solutions.

Sometimes in Small Scale Industries the production pattern undergoes a change owing to market conditions or supply position of raw materials. Hence the quality of waste water may very considerably, though not the volume. It would obviously necessitate operational adjustments in the effluent treatment plants, for which there is no in-house capability or skills in small industrial enterprises.

Obviously, availability of skilled manpower is either non-existent or if at all, it is confined to crucial and specialised production areas. It is therefore too much to expect that Small Scale Industries would employ additional and appropriately trained manpower for pollution control.

Small Scale Industries are normally dispersed except in newer industrial estates. For the joint or common treatment plant to be economically feasible, the dispersed units should come together at one place close to each other. But due to their peculiarities or locational advantages they do not want to shift. The result is that they neither put up individual treatment plants because of cost considerations, nor does the common system becomes a reality owing to distances.

At places where common treatment systems are feasible and desirable, the participating Small Scale Industries are usually unable to arrive at an agreement on the quantum of contributions towards initial investment, even where the Government is prepared to bear 50 per cent of the total required investment.

The isolated cases of community treatment plants have also failed to deliver the goods. One important amongst many reasons is the indifference and non-cooperation of participating Small Scale Industries. Also the formulae evolved for apportioning the operational expenses do not seem to be inspiring equity, justice and confidence in the members. Frequent changes, both in the quality or quantity of effluents from member unit, whether by design or otherwise, aggravate the non-co-operation further.

FINANCIAL PROBLEMS

In most cases the annualized cost of pollution control in Small Scale Industries, does not exceed 2 per cent of the sales turn over. Such costs on the face of it, may not sound too high, but converted as rupees per day, it does mean something to the entrepreneurs, who are short of cash. Fear of depressed profit margin and decline in competitiveness, therefore, makes them shun away from putting up the pollution control measures.

If the funds are available, the natural tendency is to dub the pollution control investments as a loosing proposition, an investment without returns, which is true in most cases. Obviously, entrepreneurs give preference to investments on expansional newer production facilities and other returns-oriented opportunities.

Many a times under pressure from Pollution Control Boards, some kinds of pollution control facilities are installed. Since, it costs money to operate and maintain them, the normal instinct is to keep them as show-pieces to satisfy the Board officials.

While, soft loans are made available for pollution control, the interest rate of 12.5 per cnet as against 14 per cent hardly makes them soft enough. In fact, the subsidies and other incentives offered for setting up new units are far more lucrative than what is being at present given for installation of pollution control equipment.

LACK OF MOTIVATION AND PRESSURE

Lack of awareness, ineffective regulatory approach, lack of infrastructure with law enforcing agencies, and inadequacy of financial instruments have all contributed to the climate which fosters opposition to pollution control measures. The real challenge to the environmental policy planners, therefore lies in converting the covert 'resistance' for 'pollution control' into overt 'acceptance'.

WATER POLLUTION CONTROL MEASURES IN MADURAI DISTRICT WITH REFERENCE TO THE SMALL SCALE INDUSTRIES

Generally water pollution is produced by electroplating units and cotton-dyeing units. Most of the units have not adopted water pollution control devices. Table 9.1 presents the total number of units that have treated their effluents.

Table 1

Treatment of Effluents

Sl. No.	*Name of the Industry*	*Sample Units*	*Yes*	*No*
1.	Electroplating	10	1(10.00)	9(90.00)
2.	Cotton-dyeing	19	1(5.30)	18(94.70)

Source: Survey Data.

Note: Figures In Brackets Indicate Percentages.

Of the ten electroplating units, only one has adopted water pollution control devices. It has treated its factory effluents. In some cases the effluent water is stored in number of pits inside the factory premises. After thc waste water gets evaporated, the underlying sediments are removed. Some units arrange in such a way that the waste water flows outside the factory in the evening.

The water pollution control devices are not adopted by many of the small scale polluting units due to financial restraints. The water pollution control devices require a huge investment. There are two types of costs i) Fixed cost ii) Operation cost (running).

The total investment made on water pollution control devices by electroplating and cotton-dyeing units is presented in Table 2.

Table 2

Water Pollution Control Cost

Sl. No.	*Name of the Industry*	*No. of Units*	*Fixed Cost (Rs.)*
1.	Electroplating	1	1,000
2.	Cotton-dyeing	1	1,00,000
3.	Chemical Product(sodium Alginate)	2	60,000

Source: Survey Data.

The fixed cost in water pollution control devices is very high first in the cotton-dyeing units, second in Sodium Alginate producing units and third in the electroplating units.

The State Pollution Control Board insists on the owners of the Small Scale Industries to obtain pollution clearance certificates in order to create pollution awareness in the minds of the industrialists.

The details regarding the pollution clearance certificate obtained by various polluting units are given in Table 3.

Table 3

Pollution Clearance Certificate

Sl. No.	*Name of Theindustry*	*No. of Units*	*Yes*	*No*
1.	Soap	16	1(6.30)	15(93.70)
2.	Cotton-dyeing	19	3(15.80)	16(84.20)
3.	Chemical Product	11	4(36.40)	7(63.60)
4.	Electroplating	10	3(30.00)	7(70.00)
5.	Paint	8	4(50.00)	4(50.00)

Source: Survey Data.

Note: Figures In Brackets Indicate Percentages.

Pollution clearance certificate is obtained from the State Pollution Control Board which is located in Pasumalai, Madurai. The owners of the units have to pay the prescribed amount annually for obtaining pollution clearance certificate. This amount varies from one industry to another. Of the 16 units of soap industry, only one unit has obtained pollution clearance certificate. Of the 19 units of cotton-dyeing industry, only three units have obtained pollution clearance certificate. Of the eleven units of the chemical product industry, only four units have obtained pollution clearance certifiacte. Of the ten units of the electroplating industry, only three have got the pollution clearance certificate. And of the eight units of the paint industry, only four have obtained the pollution clearance certificate.

AIR POLLUTION CONTROL MEASURES

Generally soap industry and cotton-dyeing industry create air pollution. Not even a single unit in the study area has adopted air pollution control devices, mostly because of financial constraints. In these two industries water pollution load is higher than that of air pollution and so water pollution control devices are given more importance than the air pollution control devices.

It is quite evident that the Small Scale Industries are not adopting pollution control measures. The government also is unable to thrust pollution control measures on these industries. Inability of the Small Scale Industries to adopt the prescribed pollution control measures is particularly due to financial restraints. In India, the government is not in a position to insist on the Small Scale Industries accepting pollution control policy instruments like pollution taxes, pollution permits and refundable deposits.

There are various policy instruments available to control pollution and preserve environmental quality. New methods and concepts are also being developed along with new technologies to control pollution. To choose the appropriate policy mix, efficiency, practicality and political acceptability should be considered. Obviously there are trade-offs involved and a compromise is inevitable. The provisions of the Acts should be strictly adhered to without yielding to political pressures, pressures from industries or from the public.

NOTES

1. Gursharan Varandani, "Judicial Approach to Environmental Pollution", Edited by R.K. Sapru, Environment Management in India, Vol. II, Ashish Publishing House, New Delhi, 1987, p. 125.
2. Barry Commoner, "The Social Significance of Environment Pollution", Business Economics, January 1970, p. 70.
3. Paras Diwan, "Environment and Environmental Law", Edited by Paras Diwan, Environment Protection (Problems, Policy Administration and Law), Deep and Deep Publications, New Delhi, 1987, pp. 96-97.
4. Nirmala Saraswat, "Environmental Policy for Industry in India: Present Status and Future Dimensions", Edited by Ashok Ranjan Basu and Padam Nabh Gautam, Natural Heritage of India, H.K. Publishers, Delhi, 1989, p. 38.
5. V. Joseph Xavier, S.J., "The Environmental Challenge", Paper presented at National Workshop on Aquatic Pollution, Sponsored by CSIR, Madras, October 31, 1988 to November 11, 1988, p. 4.
6. M. R. Garg and N.S. Tiwana, "The Air (Prevention and Control of Pollution) Act 1981, Lacunaes and Remedies", Paper presented in the Seminar "Environment Pollution and the Indian Scene", held at Thaper Institute of Engineering and Technology, Patiala, Feburary 28, 1986, p. 4.
7. Article 48A Inserted by Section 10 of the Constitution (Forty Second Amendment) Act, 1976.
8. G.S. Bajwa, "Problem of Environmental Pollution and its Management in India" edited by R.K. Sapru, Environment Management in India, Volume 1, Ashish Publishing House, New Delhi, 1987, p. 52.
9. Nirmala Saraswat, Op. Cit, p. 41.

10. Section 25 and 26 of the Water Act (Prevention and Control of Pollution), 1974.
11. Section 41 of the Water (Prevention and Control of Pollution) Act, 1974.
12. Section 6(6) of Environmental (Protection) Act, 1986.
13. "Crisis of Environment", The Competition Master, Chandigarh, December 1986, p. 351.
14. Government of Tamil Nadu, Tamil Nadu State Administration Report, 1986-87, pp. 122-123.
15. ISI - Indian Standard: Tolerance Limits for Industrial Effluents, 1982.
16. Yogendra N. Srivastava, Environmental Pollution, Ashish Publishing House, New Delhi, 1989, p. 65.
17. Arvill, Robert, Man and Environment: Crisis and the Strategy of Choice, Penguin Books, London, 1983, p. 339.
18. David W. Pearce and R. Kerry Turner, Economics of Natural Resources and the Environment, Harvester Wheatsheaf, Hertfordshire, 1990, p. 160.
19. J. Baumol, William and Wallace E. Oates, Economics, Environmental Policy and the Quality of Life, Prentice Hall, New Jersey, 1977, pp. 217-229.
20. Ibid., p. 2
21. M. Karpagam, Environmental Economics, Sterling Publishers, New Delhi, 1991, p. 200.
22. K.P. Nyati, Problems of Pollution and Its Control in Small Scale Industries, Friedrich Ebert Stiftung Foundation, New Delhi, pp. 13-19.

10

Findings and Recommendations

In this final chapter, an attempt is made to recapitulate the major findings arrived at in the course of the analysis made in the foregoing chapters. A few recommendations are put forward for the welfare of the workers in polluting Small Scale Industries and for the control of environmental pollution.

FINDINGS

The following are the findings relating to the growth of Small Scale Industries in terms of number of units both in Tamil Nadu as well as Madurai District in particular.

Regarding the growth of polluting Small Scale Industries in Tamil Nadu, chemical-based industries and engineering-based industries have achieved 10.01 per cent and 12.58 per cent of annual growth rates respectively, while agro-based industries and textile-based industries have achieved 16.38 per cent and 17.31 per cent of annual growth rates respectively.

Of all the polluting Small Scale Industries in Tamil Nadu, the average growth of the engineering-based industries was the highest (2300 units per annum) during 1982-91. The textile-based industries have the second highest average growth rate (1800 units per annum). The average growth of the agro-based industries occupies the third place (1600 units per annum) and the chemical- based industries are in the fourth place (1500 units per annum).

Regarding the growth of the polluting Small Scale Industries in Madurai District, agro-based industries, chemical-based industries and engineering- based industries have achieved 16.51 per cent, 18.25 per cent and 17.12 per cent of annual growth rates respectively, while textile-based industries have achieved 23.93 per cent.

Among the polluting Small Scale Industries in Madurai District, the average growth of the engineering-based industries is the highest (130 units annually) during 1982-91. The agro-based industries have the second highest average growth rate (91 units annually). The average growth rate of the textile-based industries occupies the third place (90 units annually) and the chemical-based industries are in the fourth place (66 units annually).

LOCATION AND CONCENTRATION OF SMALL SCALE INDUSTRIAL UNITS IN MADURAI DISTRICT

Periyakulam Taluk has the largest concentration of cotton-based industries. The concentration of cotton-industrial units in Andipatti Taluk is neither too high nor too low. Thirumangalam and Madurai South Taluks have average level of concentration while the other taluks namely Uthamapalayam, Vadipatti and Madurai North have a sparse distribution of units.

In the case of chemical industry in Madurai District, Vadipatti Taluk has the largest concentration. The location quotient of Madurai South Taluk is neither too high nor too low. Madurai North, Melur and Thirumangalam Taluks have average level of concentration. The other three taluks namely Usilampatti, Uthamapalayam and Periyakulam do not have sufficient share of chemical industry.

As far as the electroplating industry is concerned, Madurai South Taluk has the largest concentration of units. The other two taluks namely Madurai North and Periyakulam have low values of location quotient showing that there is a sparse distribution of units.

10.2.4. Only the following three industries-cotton-based, chemical and electroplating industries are found in Madurai South, Periyakulam and Madurai North Taluks. Particularly, concentration of the electroplating industry is high in Madurai South Taluk. Concentration of the cotton-based industries is high in Periyakulam Taluk. Normal level of concentration of chemical industry is found in Madurai North Taluk.

Only cotton-based industries and chemical industry are found in Thirumangalam, Vadipatti and Uthamapalayam Taluks. In Thirumangalam Taluk both industries have average level of concentration. In Vadipatti Taluk, chemical industry has greater concentration. In Uthamapalayam Taluk, both industries have below average level of concentration.

Madurai South Taluk ranks first in the industrial activities of Madurai District since it has the concentration of all the three industries - cotton-based, chemical and electroplating industries either at the average level or at a greater level.

PROFILE OF SAMPLE UNITS

The overall output-capital ratio of textile-based industries is Rs.15.44. The overall capital intensity in the textile-based industries works out to Rs.4,298.33. The output-labour ratio of textile-based industries as a whole is Rs.66,368.89. As far as the cotton-dyeing industry is concerned, among the ninteen units chosen, eighteen have labour productivity at a higher level than that in the whole of the textile-based industries. The average labour productivity of cotton-dyeing units is Rs.8,86,475.74. The seventeen units have capital productivity at a higher level than that in the whole of textile-based industries. The average capital productivity of cotton-dyeing units is Rs.115.41. The sixteen sample units of cotton-dyeing industry have the capital intensity at a higher level than that in the whole of the textile-based industries. The average capital intensity of cotton-dyeing units is Rs.7,680.87.

The overall output-capital ratio of chemical-based industries is Rs.6.56. The overall output-labour ratio of chemical-based industries is Rs.93,369.81. The overall capital intensity in the chemical-based industries works out to Rs.14,698.43. In the eleven sample units of the chemical product industry, the average capital productivity is Rs.16.91. The average capital intensity is Rs.42,691.57. In all the eleven sample units, labour productivity is at a higher level than that in the whole of chemical-based industries. Eight units have capital productivity at a higher level than that in the whole of the chemical-based industries. Eight units have capital intensity at a higher level than that in the whole of the chemical-based industries.

As far as the paint industry is concerned, among the eight units chosen, seven have labour productivity at a higher level than that in the whole of the chemical-based industries. The average labour productivity of the paint industry is Rs.6,41,243.48. Seven units have capital productivity at a higher level than that in the whole of the chemical-based industries. The average capital productivity of the paint industry is Rs.27.42. Six units have capital intensity at a higher level than that in the whole of the chemical-based industries. The average capital intensity in paint industry is Rs.23,384.78. The overall output-labour ratio and output-capital ratio of the chemical-based industries are Rs.93,369.81 and Rs.6.56 respectively. The overall capital intensity in the chemical-based industries works out to Rs.14,698.43.

In the case of the soap industry, among the sixteen units studied, all the units have both labour productivity and capital productivity at a higher level than that in the whole of the chemical-based industries. The average labour productivity and capital productivity of soap industry are Rs.6,16,150.35 and Rs.30.67 respectively. Among the sixteen units chosen, ten have capital intensity at a higher level than that in whole of the chemical-based industries. The average capital intensity in the soap industry is Rs.20,087.96. The overall labour productivity and capital productivity of the chemical-based industries are Rs.93,369.81 and Rs.6.56 respectively. The overall capital intensity in the chemical-based industries works out to Rs.14,698.43.

As far as the electroplating industry is concerned, among the ten units chosen as sample, all the ten have both labour productivity and capital productivity at a higher level than that in the whole of the engineering-based industries. The average labour productivity of the electroplating industry is Rs.4,01,516.21. The average capital productivity is Rs.15.21. Nine units have capital intensity at a higher level than that in the whole of the engineering-based industries. The average capital intensity in electroplating industry is Rs.26,550.13. The overall labour productivity in the engineering-based industries has been calculated to be Rs.1,24,172.55. The overall capital productivity in the engineering-based industries works out to Rs.13.52. The overall capital intensity in the engineering-based industries has been calculated to be Rs.9,183.57.

While emphasising the positive effects of the factor productivities of polluting Small Scale Industries one is aware of the negative effects which cause environmental damage. It is necessary therefore to introduce effective measures to reduce or minimise the damaging effects of pollution from the Small Scale Industries.

WATER POLLUTION

Water pollution is generated by two industries namely cotton-dyeing and electroplating. As far as cotton-dyeing industry is concerned an increase of one kilo litre of waste water would result in water pollution load of 120.590 kg in BOD and 599.640 kg in COD. There is a significant difference in water pollution load BOD and COD among the three types of cotton-dyeing units using vat dyes, naphthol dyes and direct dyes.

In the case of the electroplating industry, an increse in one kilo litre of waste water would lead to a water pollution load of 0.29 kg in BOD and 2.1 kg in COD. Comparing the influence of waste water and water pollution load in both the industries, it is higher in the cotton-dyeing industry than in the electroplating industry.

The environmental pollution is caused by the waste water of the cotton-dyeing and the electroplating units. The details regarding the total amount of the waste load in different categories of cotton-dyeing industry and electroplating industry are given in Table 1.

Table 10.1

Comparision of Permissible and Actual Waste Load

Waste in Effluent	*Type of Industries*	*Actual Waste* Load*	*Permissible Waste Load*
Bod5	Electroplating	293 Mg/L	30 Mg/L
Bod5	Naphthol Dyeing	298 Mg/L	30 Mg/L
Bod5	Vat Dyeing	124 Mg/L	30 Mg/L
Bod5	Direct Dyeing	18 Mg/L	30 Mg/L
Cod	Electroplating	2080 Mg/L	250 Mg/L
Cod	Naphthol Dyeing	1600 Mg/L	250 Mg/L
Cod	Vat Dyeing	620 Mg/L	250 Mg/L
Cod	Direct Dyeing	144 Mg/L	250 Mg/L

Note: *Waste Water In The Cotton-dyeing And The Electroplating Industries Is Tested In The Advanced Environmental Laboratory, Tamil Nadu Pollution Control Board, Pasumalai, Madurai.

From Table 1 it is evident that the total amount of the waste load calculated in different categories of the cotton-dyeing industry (naphthol dyes and vat dyes) and the electroplating industry, both BOD5 and COD exceed the tolerance limits, prescribed by the ISI as the standards for the discharage of industrial effluents (Source: IS 2490 (Part-1) - 1974 and IS 3307-1977). In the case of direct dyeing units, the waste load of BOD5 and COD is less than the tolerance limit.

AIR POLLUTION

Cotton-dyeing industry and the soap industry generate air pollution. As far as the cotton-dyeing industry is concerned an increase of output by one tonne would result in the air pollution load under different categories, — 11.1 kg, 6.3 kg, 2.2 kg, 0.1 kg and 0.6 kg, of particulates, sulphur dioxide, oxides of nitrogen, hydrocarbons and carbon monoxide respectively. When the air pollution loads under different categories among the three types of cotton-dyeing industry are converted into the load for 1000kg of output, the difference in air pollution load is insignificant.

In the case of the soap industry an increase of output by one tonne would lead to produce air pollution load under different categories - 1 kg, 1.5 kg, 0.2 kg, 0.01 kg and 0.05 kg. of particulates, sulphur dioxide, oxides of nitrogen, hydrocarbons and carbon monoxide respectively. Comparing the influence of output and air pollution load in the soap industry and the cotton-dyeing industry, it is clear that the air pollution load is heavy in the cotton-dyeing industry.

FINDINGS ON THE ENVIRONMENTAL EFFECTS OF POLLUTING SMALL SCALE INDUSTRIES ON THE WORKERS AND THE HOUSEHOLD

Nearly 58 per cent of the workers of various polluting industries suffer from different diseases like tuberculosis, stomach pain, suffocation, ulcer, skin problem, eye irritation, sore throat, asthma, headache, bronchitis and ear problem. In the case of the chemical, paint and soap manufacturing industries, the workers are affected by various occupational diseases, irrespective of any particular age group and service period. But in the case of the electroplating and the cotton-dyeing industries, the workers who have put in more than ten years of service and are above thirty years are only affected by different occupational diseases.

Waste water produced by the cotton-dyeing units and the electroplating units affect the entire household around. But in the case of paint, soap and chemical product units, the waste water pollution is not much. The quality of the ground water at Avaniapuram and Villapuram is affected and it tastes very saltish. Almost all the respondents accepted that there was definitely an impact of the waste water of the electroplating units and the cotton-dyeing units, resulting in a negative change in the environment.

Since there is no agricultural land nearby, the polluting units of the cotton-dyeing and the electroplating industries do not affect the farmers.

POLLUTION CONTROL MEASURES

The water pollution control devices are not adopted by many of the small scale polluting units in Madurai District due to financial restraints. The State Pollution Control Board insists on the owners of the Small Scale Industries for obtaining Pollution Clearance Certificates in order to create pollution awareness in the minds of the industrialists. Not even a single unit has adopted the air pollution control devices so far.

RECOMMENDATIONS

1. The lack of housing facilities for the workers and educational facilities for their childern, discourage the workers from doing their work wholeheartedly in the factories. Giving reasonable wages, providing welfare facilities and implementing other incentive schemes will improve the conditions of the workers, and make them work more effectively.
2. Scientifically tested, good quality gloves and body-covering materials should be provided by the owners of the Small Scale Industries to the workers.
3. Use of very strong chemicals should be avoided and less harmful chemicals should be used.
4. As soon as a worker is affected by a particular disease, he should immediately approach the doctor and take regular medical treatment.

5. The workers in the cotton-dyeing industry may also be provided with banana so that the dust inhaled by the workers may get dissolved.

OVERALL POLLUTION CONTROL STRATEGIES

1. To control the environmental pollution, the factories should be relocated in industrial areas. The zoning policy may be followed. The polluting units should not be situated near cultivable lands and households.
2. Those who offend the pollution control norms should be subjected to a very heavy penalty.
3. The District Pollution Control Board should also check periodically, whether the industries discharge their effluent into a stream, on land or sewer only after proper treatment.
4. Tamil Nadu Pollution Control Board should provide a mobile environmental laboratory for each district.
5. A particular industry which has effluents or air emissions would have to employ pollution control specialists to make sure that the pollution control measures are being installed and worked properly.
6. Small Scale Industries are unable to construct their own effluent treatment plant due to high cost. Hence a common effluent treatment plant is advisable.
7. A particular industry should be located in a particular area only, in order to promote common effluent treatment. Polluting Small Scale Industries should adopt single effluent treatment plant of their own. In case of economical inability, they must adopt a common effluent treatment plant. Common effluent treatment plant proposal should be encouraged by the State as well as the Central Governments through grants or subsidy. The proposal should be mainly funded by individual units. Financial institutions should offer loans at a very low rate of interest.

8. Loans for the expansion of an industry may be provided only after making sure that the particular industry would follow the necessary pollution control measures.
9. While financial incentives are given to the industries for installing pollution basement equipment, it must be carefully noted that the fight against pollution is not converted into another business, out of which a few companies would profit at the cost of the community.
10. Policies and programmes must be evolved for promoting and supporting different forms of non-polluting alternative sources of energy.
11. Some tax incentives for the Small Scale Industries which minimise pollution may be given under the Cess Act. Exemption of capital gains tax may be granted for the shifting of a polluting industry to less congested places.
12. There is an acute shortage of properly trained man power in the areas related to environmental administration. Hence proper training should be given to the persons dealing with environmental problems.
13. Central Pollution Control Board should extend assistance to the State Pollution Control Boards for training and development of man power, technical assistance and laboratory development.
14. The effort of the State to control pollution should be supplemented by efforts of individuals and other agencies. Environmental education should be imparted to the public and the public opinion against this dreadful problem should be raised.
15. It is being realised that the enactment of a code is not the ultimate solution to this multi-dimensional problem of environmental management but much depends upon those who are entrusted with the task

of implementing the provisions of such legislation. Government should take negligent officials to task who do not perform their duties to protect the environment.

16. Separate Courts or Tribunals should be established for trying cases connected with environmental pollution so that unnecessary delay is avoided, in the effective implementation of the pollution control measures by the concerned industries.
17. For mobilizing people to undertake constructive programmes aimed at environmental conservation, voluntary agencies and non-governmental organisations should be encouraged to involve themselves in fighting pollution.
18. Environmental research projects should be initiated in order to evolve new methods of environmental protection.
19. Less expensive but efficient processes for recycling of the industrial wastes should be devised.

Thus the committed efforts of industrialists, government and people would help to overcome the pollution problems created by Small Scale Industries.

Bibliography

Agarwal, S.K., and Garg, R.K., *Environmental Issues and Researches in India,* Himanshu Publications, Udaipur, 1988.

Alfred Ambasht, Weber, *Theory of Location of Industries,* English Edition by Frederick, C.J., 1949.

Ambasht, R.S., *Environment and Pollution,* Students, Friends & Co., Varanasi, 1990.

Arun C. Vakil, *Economic Aspects of Environmental Pollution in India,* Published by Arun C. Vakil, Bombay, 1984.

Arvill, Robert, *Man and Environment : Crisis and the Strategy of Choice,* Penguin Books, London, 1933.

Ashok Ranjan Basu and Padam Nabh Gautam (Ed.), *Natural Heritage of India,* H.K. Publishers, Delhi, 1989.

Atkins, M.H. and Lowe, J.F., *Pollution Control Costs in Industry - An Economic Study,* Pergamon Press, Oxford, 1977.

Batty, J., *Management Accounting,* MacDonald and Evans Ltd., London, 1970.

Baumol, J., William and Wallace E. Oates, *Economics, Environmental Policy and the Quality of Life,* Prentice Hall, New Jersey, 1977.

Benjamin, K.M.S., (Ed.), *Dimension of Environment with Special Reference to Condition in India,* Centre for Human Development and Social Change, 1971.

Bhabagrahi Misra, (Ed.), *Man, Technoloqy and Environment,* Asian Workers' Development Institute, Rourkela, 1987.

Brown M. Douglas, *Introduction to Urban Economics,* Academic Press, New York, 1974.

Chellan, M.C. and Grant, S. (Ed.), *Protecting Our Environment,* New York, 1970.

Daniel N. Lapedes, *Dictionary of Scientific and Technical Terms,* Mc-Graw Hill Publishers, 2nd Edition, New York, 1978.

David W. Pearce and Kerry Turner, R., *Economics of Natural Resources and the Environment,* Harvester, Wheatsheaf, Hertfordshire, 1990.

Desh Banthu and Eklavya Chauhan, *Current Trends in Indian Environment,* Today and Tomorrow's Printers and Publishers, New Delhi, 1977.

Dewees, D.N., Everson, C.K. and Sins, W.A., *Economic Analysis of Environmental Policies,* Toronto Press, Torontc, Canada, 1975.

Donald, T. Savage, Melril Burke, John, D. Coupe, Thomas D. Duchesneau David F. Wihry and James A. Wilson, *Economics of Environmental Improvement,* Houghton Mifflin Company, Boston, 1974.

Edward Shapiro, *Micro-Economic Analysis,* Har Court Brace Jovanrich Inc., Fourth Edition, New York, 1978.

Gadgil, P.G. and Gadgil, P.L., *Industrial Economy of India,* Eurasia Publishing House, New Delhi, 1985.

Ghanshyam N. Singh, Valuthi Varagunasingh, T., Manonmoney, N and Kanti Singh, *Environmental Economics,* Mittal Publications, New Delhi, 1991.

Godbole, M.D., *Industrial Dispersal Policies,* Himalaya Publishing House, Bombay, 1979.

Gunnar Myrdal, *Asian Drama,* An Inquiry into the Poverty of Nations, Vol. II, Kalyani Publishers, New Delhi, 1985.

Gupta, N.S. and Amarjit Singh, *Industrial Economy of India,* Light and Life Publishers, New Delhi, 1978.

Howard E. Hesketh, *Understanding and Controlling Pollution,* Ann Arbor Science Publishers Inc., Michigan, U.S.A., 1973.

Hunt Williams and Donaldson, *Basic Business Finance,* Richard D. Irwin Inc., Home Wood Illinois, 1971.

Inderjeet Sethi, Sethi, M.S. and Sethi, S.A., *Environmental Pollution, Causes, Effects and Control, Air Pollution and Human Health,* Common Wealth Publishers, New Delhi, 1991.

Jana, M.M., *Environmental Degradation and Developmental Strategies in India,* Ashish Publishing House, New Delhi, 1991.

Karpagam, M., *Environmental Economics,* Sterling Publishers, New Delhi, 1991.

Kendrick, John, W. and Geamer Daniel, *Measuring Company Productivity,* New York, 1961.

Khoshoo, T.N., *Environmental Concerns and Strategies,* Ashish Publishing House, New Delhi, 1988.

Mahajan, V.S., (Ed.), *Studies in Energy and Economic Development,* Deep & Deep Publications, New Delhi, 1991.

Manivasakam, N., *Industrial Effluents – Origin, Characteristics, Effects, Analysis and Treatment,* Sakthi Publications, Coimbatore, 1987.

Melvin Greenhut, *Plant Location in Theory and Practice,* The University of North Carolian Press, 1956.

Michael Roysten, *Pollution Prevention Pays,* Pergamon Press, Oxford, 1979.

Mohan, I., *Environmental Pollution and Management,* Ashish Publishing Company, New Delhi, 1989.

Nyati, K.P., *Problems of Pollution and Its Control in Small Scale Industries,* Friedrich Ebert Foundation, New Delhi, 1988.

Paras Diwan, *Environment Protection (Problems, Policy Administration and Law),* Deep and Deep Publications, New Delhi, 1987.

Perumalsamy, S., *Economic Development of Tamil Nadu,* S. Chand & Company Limited, New Delhi, 1990.

Pramod Singh, (Ed.), *Ecology of Rural India,* Ashish Publishing House, New Delhi, 1987.

Rice Odell, Environmental Awakening : *The New Revolution to Protect the Earth,* Balinger Publishing & Co., Cambridge, 1980.

Sapru, R.K. (Ed.), *Environment Management in India,* Vol. I and II, Ashish Publishing House, New Delhi, 1987.

Sargant Florence, P., *Investment. Location and Size of Plant,* Cambridge, 1948.

Sargant Florence, P. *The Logic of British and American Industry,* London, 1961.

Sargant Florence, P., *The Logic of British and American Industries,* Routedge and Organ Paul Ltd., London, 1972.

Sastry, N.S.R., *A Statistical Study of India's Industrial Development,* Thacker & Co., Bombay, 1943.

Speight, H., *Economics and Industrial Efficiency, An Introduction to Managerial Economics,* Macmillan, Third Edition, New Delhi, 1970.

Sreekantaradhya, *Regional Dispersal of Industries and Industrial Development,* Deep and Deep Publications, New Delhi, 1985.

Timmy Katyal and Sataka, M., *Environmental Pollution,* Anmol Publications, New Delhi, 1990.

Trivedy, R.K., *Ecology and Pollution of Indian Rivers,* Ashish Publishing House, New Delhi, 1988.

Tulsi Ram Sharma and Singh Chauhan, S.D., *Industrial Economics,* Shiva Lal Agarwala and Company, Agra, 1972.

Uma Maheswara Rao, C.H., *Small Scale Industries Economic Aspects,* Popular Prakashan, Bombay, 1965.

Vakil, C.N. (Ed.), *Location of Industry: Evolution of a Policy in Industrial Development in India,* Orient Longman, 1973.

Wilfrid Bach, *Atmospheric Pollution,* McGraw-Hill Book Company, New York, 1989.

Yogendra N. Srivastava, *Environmental Pollution,* Ashish Publishing House, New Delhi, 1989.

JOURNALS

Arun Kumar Bhatt, "Dangerous Work" , *The Hindu Survey of Environment,* 1993.

Barry Commoner, "The Social Significance of Environment Pollution", *Business Economics,* January, 1970.

Baruch Fischhoff, "Science and Politics in the Midst of Environmental Disaster", Heldref Publications, Washington, *Environment,* Vol. 33, No.2, March, 1991.

Biman Basu, "Environment Protection : A Many Faceted Problem", *Current Topics,* Ambala Cantt, July, 1986.

"Crisis of Environment", *The Competition Master,* Chandigarh, December, 1986.

"Draft Policy Statement on Pollution Control in India", *World Focus,* Vol. 12, No.1, January, 1991.

Dunu Roy, "Occupational Hazards, When the Grind Tells on You", *The Hindu Survey of the Environment,* Vol. 57, 1993.

Gaensler, E.A., "Environmental Lung Disease", *Medical Clinics of North America,* Vol. 57, 1973.

Government of India, *Economic Survey,* 1991-92.

Hawkins, L.C., "Measurement of Efficiency", *Oxford Economic Papers,* New Series, Vol. 11, No.1, 1950.

Kalyanasundaram, N., "Facing Threat on Several Fronts", *The Hindu Survey of the Environment,* 1991.

Madras Institute of Development Studies, *Bulletin,* March, 1993.

Malleswara Rao, M., "Andhra Pradesh - A Growing Industrial Monster", *The Hindu Survey of the Environment,* 1991.

Mehta, M.C., "Taj Trapezium: A Wonder under Smog", *The Hindu Survey of the Environment,* 1994.

Munim, A.V., "Combating Air Pollution – Mission Impossible'?", *Chemical Engineering World,* Vol. VII, No.11, November, 1972.

Neena, Vyas, "In the Pollution Capital", *The Hindu Survey of the Environment,* 1991.

Ramakrishnan, N., "Madras: Troubled Giant of South", *The Hindu Survey of the Environment,* 1992.

Ramdas, N. , "The Fly Ash Menace", *The Hindu Survey of the Environment,* 1991.

Ramesh Upadhyaya, "Big Problems of Chotanagpur", *The Hindu Survey of the Environment,* 1991.

Roy Mathew, "Kerala - A Controversial Project", *The Hindu Survey of the Environment,* 1991.

Sampath, R., "Potentially Explosive Visakhapatnam", *The Hindu Survey of the Environment,* 1992.

Sandesara, J.C., "Modern Small Industry, 1972 and 1987-88 Aspects of Growth and Structural Change", *Economic and Political Weekly,* Vol. XXVIII, No.6, February 6, 1993.

Sastry, C.A., Alagarswamy, S.R. and Kothandaraman, V., "Treatment of Paper and Wastes-A Case Study", *Indian Journal of Environmental Health,* Vol. 16, No.4, October, 1974.

Schilling, R.S., "Byssinosis in Textile Industry", *Journal of Environmental Health,* Vol. 21, 1970.

Sreenivasan, A. and Sounderraj, R., "Effects of Certain Wastes on the Water Quality and Fisheries of Rivers Cauvery and Bhavani", *Environmental Health,* Vol. 9, 1967.

Sushil Kumar, A. , "Towards Strict Liability", *Economic Times,* 2 February, 1986.

Times of India, May 27, 1987.

WHO, *World Health,* May 1972.

REPORTS / SEMINAR AND WORKSHOP PAPERS

Adinarayana Reddy, K., "Environmental Issues and Planning Considerations: A Case Study of Calcutta", Calcutta Metropolitan Development Authority, C.M.D. Information, 1984.

CMDA, "C.M.D. Information", Calcutta, 1984.

Department of Environment and Forests and Wild Life, "Parayavaran Abstracts", Environmental Information System, Vol.II, New Delhi, 1985.

Evaluation and Applied Research Department, Tamil Nadu-An Economic Appraisal, Madras, December, 1994.

Founex Report, "Development and Environment", Digest, 10, 1972.

Garg, M.R. and Tiwana, N.S., "The Air (Prevention and Control of Pollution) Act, 1981, Lacunas and Remedies", Paper presented in the Seminar "Environment Pollution and the Indian Scene", held at Thaper Institute of Engineering and Technology, Patiala, February 28, 1986.

Government of India, Small Scale Industries Hand Book of Statistics, Small Scale Industries, New Delhi, 1973.

Government of Tamil Nadu, Action for 1985-88, Department of Industries and Commerce, Madurai District, District Industries Centre, Madurai.

ISI - Indian Standard: Tolerance Limits for Industrial Effluents, 1982.

Joseph Xavier. V, S.J., "The Environmental Challenge", Paper Presented at National Workshop on Aquatic Pollution, Sponsored by CSIR, Madras, October 31, 1988 to November 11, 1988.

Karnataka Legislative Assembly, Report of the Committee on Government Assurances to Legislative Assembly on Industrial Pollution, Bangalore, 1976.

Kothari, J.C., "Lung Disease in Industry", Paper presented in the National Seminar on "Industry, Environment and Man", Organised by The Central Labour Institute and the Society for Clean Environment, Bombay, 8-9, February, 1975.

Krishnamurti, R., "Kaveri Basin Economic Development", Workshop conducted on behalf of The Department of Environment, Government of India, Science Foundation, Madras.

Manonmoney, N., "Environmental Problems in Developed Countries", Paper presented in the United Nations Environmental Programme, held in Madurai Kamaraj University, Madurai, 18-22, December, 1989.

Planning Commission, Second Five Year Plan, 1956-1961.

Shahul Hameed, M., "A Report on the Hydrobiological Conditions of the River Cauvery and the Industrial Effluents in and around Tamil Nadu", Memoirs of the Salem Institute of Experimental Biology, No.1, 1981.

SIDCO, Annual Report, 1991-92.

Small Industries Service Institute, Tamil Nadu - A Profile, 1992.

Tamil Nadu State Administration Report, Government of Tamil Nadu, 1986-87.

The Constitution Act, 1976, Article 48A, Section 10 (Forty Second Amendment).

The Environmental (Protection Act), 1986, Section 6 (6).

The Water Act (Prevention and Control of Pollution), 1974, Section 25 and 26.

The Water Act (Prevention and Control of Pollution), 1974, Section 41.

Tinbergen, "Reshaping the International Order", A Report to the Club of Rome, 1976.

Tiwari, T.N. and Manzoor Ali, "Water Quality Index for Indian Rivers", Rourkela, 1982.

THESES

Abubacker, M.H., "Socio-Economic Impact of Pollution: A Study of Cement Factories in Tiruchirapalli District, Tamil Nadu", Unpublished Ph.D. Thesis, Bharathidasan University, Tiruchirapalli, 1990.

Backyavathy, D.M., "Epidemiological, Environmental and Toxicological Studies on Tannery and Chromate Industrial Workers of Ranipet Industrial Town and Its Environs", Unpublished Ph.D. Thesis, S.V. University, Tirupati, 1986.

Baskaran, M., "Environmental Impact of Cement Industry with Reference to Madras Cements Limited", Unpublished M.Phil. Thesis, School of Economics, Madurai Kamaraj University, Madurai, 1992.

Edward Benjamin, R., "Economics of Leather Industry of Tamil Nadu with Special Emphasis on East India

Leathers", Unpublished Ph.D. Thesis, School of Economics, Madurai Kamaraj University, February, 1979.

Mariappan, M., "A Study of Environmental Pollution in Madurai City", Unpublished M.Phil. Thesis, School of Economics, Madurai Kamaraj University, Madurai, April, 1990.

Ramasubramanian, A., "Health Conditions of Workers – An Assessment Based on Dust Pollution in India Cements Limited, Sankar Nagar, Nellai Kattabomman District", Unpublished Thesis, School of Economics, Madurai Kamaraj University, Madurai, April, 1990.

Ushakumary, K., "A Study of the Linkages of Electrical Machinery Industry in Kerala", Unpublished Ph.D. Thesis, Department of Applied Economics, University of Science and Technology, Cochin, 1992.